＊ INSIGHT POCKET GUIDES

aegean
ISLANDS
MYKONOS & SANTORINI

D0071598

APA PUBLICATIONS
Part of the Langenscheidt Publishing Group

L

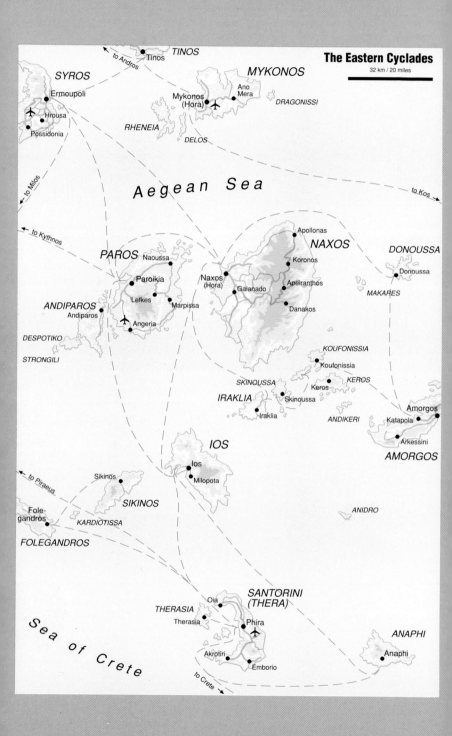

Welcome!

The people of the Cyclades have proven themselves true alchemists in the decades since World War II: they have turned the barren stones upon which they live into 24-carat gold. Some lament the islands' loss of innocence, but for anyone who has never been there before, the Cyclades will be as young and fresh as Aphrodite on her half-shell, and every bit as seductive.

In these pages, Insight Guides' expert on the region, Elizabeth Boleman-Herring, has designed a series of tours to help you make the most of a one- to two-week stay on the key Cycladic islands of Mykonos and Santorini, with possible side-trips to the holy isle of Delos, Naxos, Paros and Andiparos. The book is arranged as a series of routes, which take in the best of the sights but still leave time for sunning and swimming. Supporting the itineraries are sections on shopping and eating out, in which the author shares her own favourite recommendations, plus a fact-packed practical information section.

 Elizabeth Boleman-Herring has written seven books on Greece (including *Insight Pocket Guide: Athens*) and has lived and worked on Mykonos and Santorini. It gives her great pleasure to act as your guide, and she hopes this book will prove both a practical and inspiring companion. With her help, the images you take home — of snowy whitewash smelling of lime and the sea, of jasmine and hibiscus and bougainvillaea on the curving walls, of red mullet and octopus smoking over coals — will remain, as clear as the Aegean Sea or unwatered ouzo.

C O N T E N T S

History & Culture

Stepping stones between East and West, the Aegean Islands (the Cyclades) have witnessed a long succession of traders and invaders, from the ancient Dorians to German fascists in World War II

Pages 2/3:
Island idyll

Santorini's Highlights

Four itineraries focusing on popular Santorini.

Pages 8/9: Harbour at Naoussa

Shopping and Eating Out

Calendar of Events

Practical Information

Maps

HÍSTORY &

The Cyclades, all 30 or 40 stony, white knucklebones haphazardly tossed upon Homer's wine-dark Aegean Sea, are well-named. Feminine nouns one and all, their names are pure poetry. In fact, Greece's Nobel Prize-winning poet, Odysseus Elytis, simply ticks off a catalogue of them in his great poem, *Axion Esti*, with little need for narrative: they sing off the page. Mykonos, Sikinos, Serifos, Folegandros, Andiparos, Despotiko, Anaphi, Poliegos, et cetera. For Greeks and philhellenes alike, Greece *is* the islands, and the islands are Greece. Once seen, once visited, they engender a longing that no other place on earth can satisfy. Once beguiled by what Mykonos' enticing, pink twilight does for the human face, or stunned by Santorini's brutal grandeur, you will find you must return.

Pronounced *Sic-luh-deez* in English, the island group's name derives from *kyklos*, the Greek word for 'circle' and the root of such

Civilisations of the past

Culture

Ancient octopus vase

English words as cyclone and cycle. Scattered in the middle of the Aegean, the Cyclades encircle Delos, the holy island of antiquity, which was already a flourishing shrine in the second millennium BC, and revered as the birthplace of the Olympian god of light and learning, Apollo.

But the importance of the Cyclades antedates both the Mycenaean and Athenian ascendencies, and even the much earlier Minoan. First visited by immigrants from the East, the Carians, the Cyclades' pivotal geographical location sealed their fate: the Cyclades were destined for very early greatness indeed, as a series of stepping stones between East and West.

Early Bronze Age sailors, instrument-poor and loth to leave the sight of land, used these marble outcroppings in the sea as way-stations en route from Ionia to mainland Greece. The Cycladic ship-builders and 'merchant seamen' of the third millennium BC had much in common with the insular Greeks of today. In many important ways, life has not changed here in some 7,000 years of unbroken habitation. Then, as now, the long, sultry summers were the time for travel, for trade and communication with the shores beyond, though the *meltemi*, a fierce summer gale that blows today's travellers' plans to the four winds, capsized the ancients' vessels as well. Wet, windy winters kept, and keep, Cycladic seamen port-bound from November to March, when storms make sailing treacherous.

Links with the Past

Even the diet in the Cyclades has changed little since farming was first introduced in 6000BC, and permanent habitation became possible on these relatively inhospitable islands of schist, granite and marble. There is evidence of Neolithic settlements on Saliagos (Snail islet) and Keos dating from 5000BC. Tiny Saliagos, once part and par-

11

Early Cycladic sculpture

cel of an island comprising Paros and Andiparos as well, was the earliest Cycladic settlement. Here, archaeologists found a group of small dry-stone-walled dwellings, and marble figurines, one an abstract idol of the 'violin type'; the other 'steatopygous' or, in other words, a 'fat-bottomed lady': the first examples of the highly sophisticated and stylised Early Cycladic art which now graces the collections of the British Museum and the Goulandris Museum of Cycladic and Ancient Greek Art in Athens.

The contemporary jewellery collections of Lalaounis and Zolotas, modern Greece's best known goldsmiths, still feature many of these appealing forms in silver and gold: Cycladic abstraction is as eloquent now, in a new translation, as it was then. Then, as now, the inhabitants of the Cyclades possessed a heightened appreciation for clean lines, for forms stripped of decoration and trivial embellishment. The architecture of Mykonos' main town, the stark simplicity of Tinos's dovecotes and chapels, the Stone Age elegance of Andros's schist walls, the sculptural evolution (eventually) of any and all Cycladic corners into curves – under unremitting generations of whitewash – there is a striking continuity between the marbles of the Early Cycladic masters and the vernacular expressions of their heirs (though fat-bottomed ladies are no longer in vogue on Mykonian and Parian shores).

Lawrence Durrell, writing about the Greek islands he loved, attributed this consistency to the natural forces which have shaped and sculpted the islands and islanders for seven millennia: 'All habits, of course, stem from climate which, in a subtle, unobtrusive manner, dictates everything about the way we live, and often about the way we love.' Climate: the sea, the sun, and the wind. For the Carians, as well as for the Cycladic islanders of today – living at the edge of a sea full of gifts; backlit by an omnipotent, omnipresent sun; feeding on the philosopher's diet of goat cheese, grain, grapes, olives, figs and fresh fish; buffeted by a soul-purifying wind – climate has engendered a particular way of being, and of looking at the world, a way that continues to seduce.

Violent Origins

Despite their common Bronze Age culture and present-day similarities, though, the Cyclades have, individually, marched to somewhat different drummers due to the vicissitudes of stormy Aegean history. The Dorians, the Romans, the Byzantines, Venetians, Genoese, Ottoman Turks, Russians, German fascists, and pirates of all persuasions have led these pretty (sitting) ducks a merry chase, and the architecture and ethnic make-up of each island reflects even now the influences of visitors benign and barbaric. However, Santorini, known to the Greeks as Thera, is unique. It is the sole member of the group to have been blown to smithereens and lived to tell the tale. Once a huge, fertile island, circular in shape, and known to the ancients as *Kalliste* (The Beautiful) and *Strongyle* (The Round), Santorini gave rise to the sophisticated and highly evolved civilisation of Akrotiri, which flourished from 2000–c.1628BC. Akrotiri, which has been preserved for us just as Pompeii and Herculaneum were preserved, in the 'amber' of molten lava and blankets of pumice and ash, fell victim to a violent volcanic explosion that blew 36 cubic miles of matter sky-high, and left the formerly round isle a jagged crescent moon without a centre. Life on Bronze Age Santorini ended with the cataclysm, but the eruption carved an eerily compelling landscape that rivals any in the world for drama. It was not until circa 300BC that another culture rose on Thera, when the Ptolemies established a Hellenistic stronghold atop lofty Mesa Vouno (Ancient Thera), but for all time to come, Santorini's vertiginous cliffs, its awesome caldera – the great bay formed when the volcano blew its top – and the crater still smoking in water 80°C (176°F) would demand the world's uneasy attention.

Santorini and Mykonos

Santorini today, with Anaphi the southernmost of the major Cyclades, is perhaps the most popular destination in the Mediterranean in high season. Windsurfers and sunbathers throng the black volcanic beaches on the east coast, and though the capital, Phira, is boisterously packed during July and August, the island's 14 lovely, diverse villages seem easily to swallow up the crowds. While the young come for the party, and the heady and justly famous white Santorini wines, nevertheless the antiquities and architecture, prehistoric, Byzantine,

Santorini painting, 1866

Traditional dress in a Nationalist painting

Veneto-Catholic and troglodytic (barrel and cross-vaulted dwellings dug out of the volcanic earth) attract more cerebral visitors.

The excavations at Akrotiri, on Thera's southern coast, begun in 1967 by Professor Spyridon Marinatos (crushed by falling debris on the site on 1 October 1974 and laid to rest within his beloved Bronze Age town), warrant several return visits. A stop at the National Archaeological Museum is in order before setting out for Santorini, however, as the 'frescoes' so carefully removed from Akrotiri's walls are ensconced in a climate-controlled room in the capital city. These elaborate paintings reflect a cultural complexity as striking as that of Minoan Knossos. Phantasmagorical fauna, graceful deer and dancing swallows, bare-breasted priestesses carrying incense, and a vast, multi-oared fleet of Akrotirian vessels bespeak a bourgeois, moneyed, urban and wide-ranging Bronze Age sea power, organized under a central authority able to undertake public works such as a city sewage system. Yet, in contrast to Pompeii, not one body has been found in the shattered city. Professor Christos Doumas, the current director of the dig, assures us that while Akrotiri perished, the Akrotirians, apparently to a man, escaped with all their valuables. Alerted by tremors and preliminary eruptions, the seamen took to the sea, fleeing the devastation in their graceful 30m (100ft) ships.

Mykonos' history, though certainly less cataclysmic, reads like a biblical catalogue of conquerors, each begetting a successor until the island was appropriated, for good, following World War II, by artists, sun-seekers and international hedonists. However, the architecture of the harbour town and island capital, Hora, reflects the Mykonians' abiding unwillingness to give up without a fight. That skein of tangled streets, in which even long-time residents can take a wrong turning, was constructed primarily to confuse pirates such as Barbarossa who, despite any confusion, seized Mykonos in 1537. But neither the wind nor marauders have ever penetrated

14

Hora's defences easily. Ironically, in antiquity, no one en route to neighbouring Delos (where, during the Hellenistic Era, on a bullish day, 10,000 slaves might change hands in the great slave market) gave Mykonos a second look. Today, poppies, wild asparagus and armies of lizards inhabit the rich ruins of Delos, and all that glitters is located across the windy channel on Mykonos.

Few today visit Mykonos because of its proximity to Delos, though daily caiques ferry earnest antiquarians across the treacherous straits, about a half-hour passage. Nor is the untutored eye capable of picking out neolithic sites on Mykonos, though they exist, nor of identifying architectural vestiges of the Saracen, Catalan, Turkish, Byzantine, Venetian, and Russian occupations. Four fine museums on the island partially remedy this situation, though the Archaeological Museum's collection consists primarily of finds from the islet of Rheneia, whence all Delian graves were removed in 426–5BC. An exception is the massive relief amphora depicting the Trojan War. This 7th-century BC masterpiece, unearthed in Hora, will have been used for a burial, but Mykonos cannot claim its maker: the piece was made in a workshop on the island of Tinos.

Even Mykonos' revolutionary war heroine, Mando Mavrogennous was an import. Born in Trieste in 1796, she was the descendant of an illustrious emigré family which had fled Constantinople for the Cyclades, and granddaughter of Dimitrios Mavrogennous, councillor and voivode of Mykonos. Heir to a fortune, Mando was gently reared, multilingual and musical, but fearlessly committed to the cause of liberty, or death, for the Greeks suffering under the Ottoman yoke. In 1821, when the Hellenes rose against their masters, Mando sailed for Mykonos. In October of the following year, when the Turks attacked her adopted isle, she led the Mykonian militia, successfully routing the fierce adversaries. To the

Mando Mavrogennous

last drachma, Mando poured out her fortune for the war effort, outfitting ships, purchasing arms and relieving the suffering of the refugees. Dressed in male attire, she led the troops on Mykonos, Evia and in Thessaly, and was awarded the rank of general by the General Assembly at Nauplia following the successful outcome of the revolution. She died on Paros in 1848, a poor relation of her Parian family. Today, busts of the heroine stand watch over tourists' rucksacks and the fleet of taxis on Mykonos, and strollers in the main square of Paroikia on Paros. Both islands claim her as their own.

Other Islands

The Cyclades today are breathtakingly diverse, tirelessly welcoming. They range from lush, well-watered Andros, home of wealthy shipowners and the Goulandris family's matchless museums to little windswept Anaphi, where the Monastery of the Kalamiotissa welcomes modern argonauts just as its rocky shores once sheltered Jason of the Golden Fleece. Mountainous, fertile Naxos, the largest of the group, is studded with reminders of its medieval past as the glorious seat of Marco Sanudo, the 13th-century Duke of the Archipelago, and nephew of Venice's doge. It was on Naxos that Theseus, the mythological slayer of King Minos's Minotaur, either deserted Ariadne, the Cretan king's daughter, or lost her to the god Dionysos. The fertility of Naxian soil supports the latter version: Dionysos was the god of wine.

Amorgos boasts the most beautiful monastery in the Aegean — whitewashed Khozoviotissa, clinging to the naked cliffs like a nesting gull. Tinos, the Hellenic Lourdes, has usurped Delos's role as Greece's holy isle, and the 15 August observance of the Dormition of the Virgin rivals any in the world for piety and solemnity. Syros is home to confectioners, Greek Catholics, merchant seamen and the nome's (provincial) government offices. Sifnos and Serifos are relatively untouched as yet by foreign visitation, so remain the Cycladic favourites of young Athenians on holiday. And Paros, source of the translucent, snowy marble used for the Aphrodite of Milos and birthplace of Archilochus (c720–c640BC), the first master of the lyric poem, may be the quintessential Cycladic isle. Here are a windmill à la Mykonos, blue domes atop whitewashed walls reminiscent of Santorini, Greece's oldest church (the Ekatontapyliani, founded by the Emperor Justinian) and, of course, nudist beaches, nightclubs, temple ruins, sea caves, olive groves, and everything else a guest, whether Bronze Age, or bronzed age, could desire.

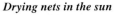

Drying nets in the sun

Historical Highlights

8000BC Milos trades obsidian throughout Aegean.

3200–2000 Early Bronze Age heyday of Cycladic culture.

3000 Oared vessels in use by Cycladic sailors, also the first Greeks to add keels to their ships.

c2600–1400 Ascendency of Crete's Minoan *thalassocracy*.

c1628 Santorini (Thera) explodes in cataclysmic volcanic eruptions. Theran civilisation at Akrotiri ends.

c1250–40 The Trojan War.

c1115 Dorians capture Santorini.

1100–800 After the decline of Mycenaean civilisation, mainlanders emigrate south and east, revitalising the islands.

825 Phoenician alphabet introduced on Santorini, Milos, Crete.

776 First Olympic Games held.

c750 Homer composes *Iliad* and *Odyssey*.

c716 Archilochus, first lyric poet, born on Paros.

540 Under Peiseistratos, erection of an archaic temple to Apollo on Delos and removal of graves.

479 Greeks send fleet assembled at Delos to Asia Minor, defeating Persians at Mykale.

477 Athens establishes Delian League, its treasury and headquarters located on Delos.

470–69 Naxos's attempt to secede from Delian League brutally quashed by Athens.

454 League's treasury removed from Delos to Athens.

428–347 Plato refers to the 'lost kingdom of Atlantis' – more likely Minoan Crete than Santorini.

426–5 Second 'purification' of Delos; graves removed to Rheneia.

405 Sparta seizes control of the Aegean.

323 Death of Alexander the Great.

146 Greece becomes a Roman province.

88 King Mithridates of Pontus sacks Delos.

69 Delos's final destruction by the pirate Athenodorus.

c95AD St John the Divine dictates *Revelation* on Patmos.

330 The Emperor Constantine establishes Constantinople as capital of the New Rome.

1095 Christian Crusades begin.

1204 Constantinople falls to Franks and Venetians; Venetian Marco Sanudo seizes Naxos; creates the Duchy of the Archipelago.

1210 Aegean isles parcelled out amongst the leaders of the Fourth Crusade.

1292 Spanish Admiral Roger de Lluria attacks Naxos, Andros, Tinos, Kythnos and Chios.

1453 Turks capture Constantinople.

1566 Delos occupied by Turkish pirates.

1615 Semi-autonomous and democratic Community of Mykonos established.

1684 War between the Ottoman Turks and Venice.

1803 Hydra establishes an armed fleet to rout pirates.

1820 Venus de Milo (the Aphrodite of Milos) removed to the Louvre by a French officer.

25 March 1821 National Independence Day: Greeks initiate hostilities against the Turks.

1827 At the Battle of Navarino, the Ottoman-Egyptian fleet is routed by the British, French and Russians.

1828 Southern Greece, the Sporades and Cyclades proclaimed free.

1848 Mando Mavrogennous dies on Paros.

1877 French School of Archaeology begins Delian excavations.

1896–1901 Hiller von Gaertringen excavates on Santorini.

1912–13 Dodecanese occupied by Italy following Italo-Turkish War; northern Aegean islands ceded to Greece by Turkey after Second Balkan War.

1944–7 British occupy the Dodecanese, which become the last Aegean territory to be added to the modern Greek state.

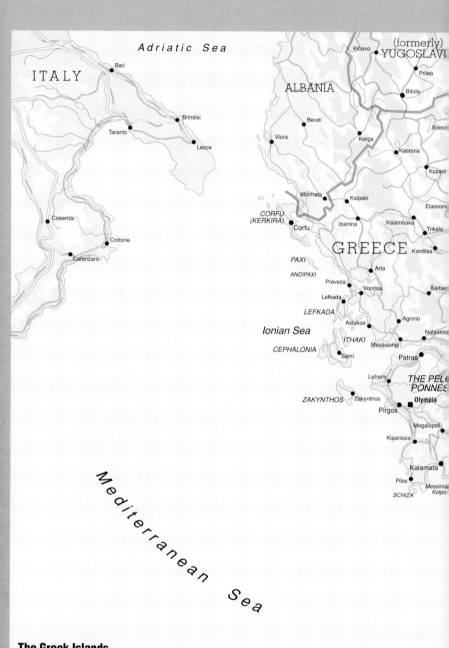

The Greek Islands

120 km / 75 miles

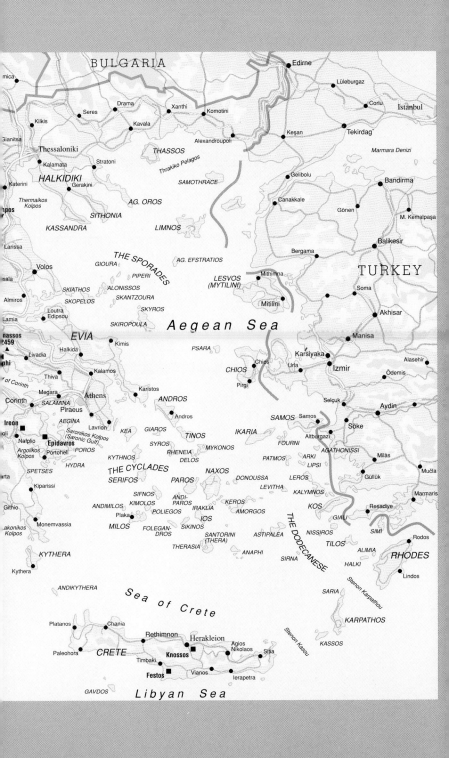

Day itine.
Mykonos

Though some visitors fly into Mykonos by summer charter flights from northern Europe, most proceed to Athens by air first. Unless your time is limited, I'd suggest you spend a night in Athens prior to setting out, by steamer from Piraeus, for Mykonos. Ferries depart at around 8am and arrive at Hora, Mykonos at 2pm. First class cabins make the trip cool and restful: in high season, there may even be live classical music in the first class lounge, though the bar serves only mediocre snacks. Reserve hotel accommodation in advance via fax or telex, and ask your hotelier to meet your ferry. The arrivals pier, and the Olympic Airways bus terminus, are chaotic places to arrange transport, May through September. (The fastest route to Mykonos is via Olympic Airways to Athens and then straight on, via Olympic, to the island. Check your luggage through and proceed to the domestic gates without exiting transit. Your hotelier, if faxed, will meet the flight.)

Classic Mykonos

1. Town, Beach and Nightlife

A full day (not Monday). Early breakfast at L'Angolo Bar in Hora; on foot from the crossroads of the Plati Yialos/Ornos roads, southeast towards the cemetery and School of Fine Arts on Aghiou Ioannou Street; a working windmill and the Archaeological Museum; down Hora's Matoyianni Street; Nikos (Skepathianos) Fish-taverna for lunch. Afternoon swim at Plati Yialos, Psarrou or Paranga beaches; dinner at Katrin's, Sesame Kitchen or La Bussola; dancing at the Mykonos Club or Astra Bar; quiet, late-night drinks at the Veranda (Green House) bar.

If you are staying at one of the hotels near the crossroads, it's a one-minute walk to the starting point in the Maouna area of Hora. Ask your concierge for directions. To reach the **L'Angolo Bar** for breakfast, head downhill towards Hora from the Maouna crossroads. Enter the lopsided square where the turquoise Ornos/Plati Yialos/Paradise Camping buses terminate, and bear right down Aghiou Louka

Windmills at breakfast

Street, taking a sharp right turning just before the pharmacy: you should now be able to smell L'Angolo's Italian roast coffee, brewing in a tiny coffee bar immediately on your left. (This is Hora's Lakka district.)

From the Maouna crossroads, after breakfast, proceed in a southeasterly direction on Aghiou Ioannou Street towards the church of Aghios Loukas (St Luke), and Hora's main cemetery, both on your left a few metres from the crossroads. Be very careful on this busy road: first-time motor-scooterists abound in wobbly confusion. A minute or so further on, on your right behind a blue door in a white Cycladic wall, is Mykonos' School of Fine Arts. (Artists interested in temporary studio space at the school should contact

Mrs Maria Lapourta in Athens; tel: 363 4751.) Pass the gym, which offers aerobics, weightlifting, body building, saunas, etc, on your right, and the road curves gently to the left. On your left, white walls and cubistic villas are festooned with crimson bougainvillaea. Prickly pears, oleander bushes, fig, eucalyptus, lemon and almond trees and reeds round out Mykonos' limited but appealing flora. A modern

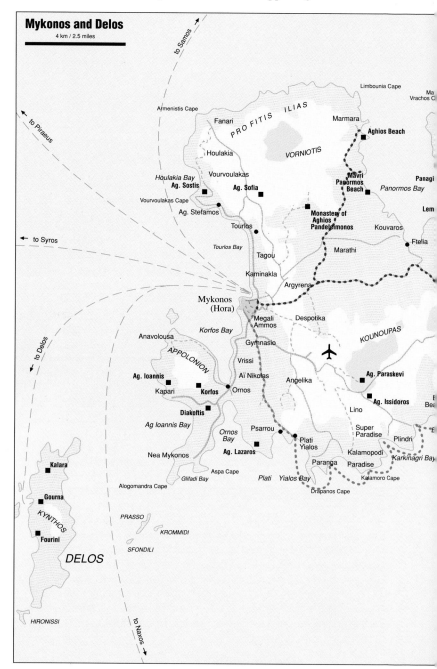

Mykonos and Delos

4 km / 2.5 miles

to Samos

to Piraeus

to Syros

to Delos

Limbounia Cape

Ma Vrachos C

Armenistis Cape

Fanari

PROFITIS ILIAS

Marmara

Aghios Beach

Houlakia

VORNIOTIS

Houlakia Bay

Vourvoulakas

Panagi

Ag. Sostis

Ag. Sofia

Mavri Panormos Beach

Panormos Bay

Vourvoulakas Cape

Ag. Stefamos

Monastery of Aghios Pandeleimonos

Lem

Tourlos

Kouvaros

Ftelia

Tourlos Bay

Tagou

Marathi

Kaminakla

Argyrena

Mykonos (Hora)

Megali Ammos

Despotika

KOUNOUPAS

Korfos Bay

Anavolousa

Gymnasio

APPOLONION

Vrissi

Ag. Ioannis

Aï Nikolas

Angelika

Ag. Paraskevi

Kapari

Korfos

Ornos

Ag. Issidoros

Diakoftis

Lino

Bea

Ag Ioannis Bay

Ornos Bay

Psarrou

Super Paradise

Plindri

Nea Mykonos

Ag. Lazaros

Plati Yialos

Kalamopodi

Karkinagri Bay

Kalara

Aspa Cape

Paranga

Paradise

Glifadi Bay

Plati Yialos Bay

Kalamoro Cape

Alogomandra Cape

Drapanos Cape

Gourna

KYNTHOS

PRASSO

Fourini

KROMMIDI

SFONDILI

DELOS

HIRONISSI

to Naxos

dovecote or two may catch your eye: reminders of the Cyclades' Venetian heritage. As you climb higher, the view of Hora deepens below you, a scene that takes in the pretty islands of Rheneia and Delos in the middle distance, behind the chapel-topped islet of Baou; Tinos, usually draped in fleecy cloud, lies to your right directly beyond the beach community of San Stefanos.

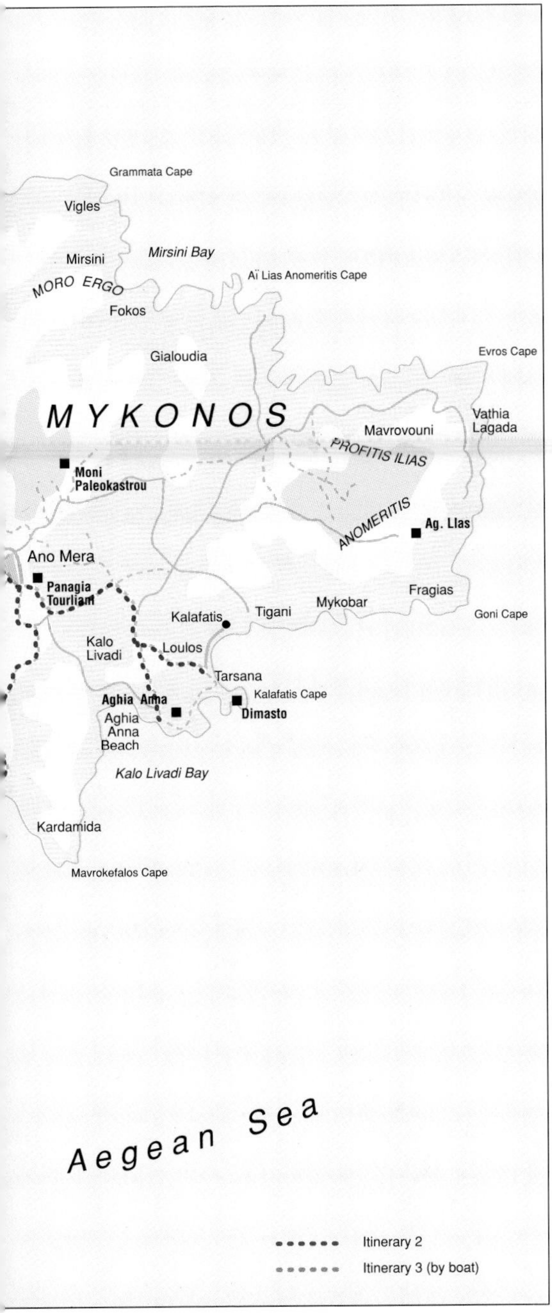

If you want to climb still higher, take the first turning to the right and wind back and forth on the Ano Mera village/Kalafatis beach road, till you reach a thatchless windmill. Otherwise, proceed along Aghiou Ioannou Street till you reach Hora's sole working **windmill**, part of Mykonos' **Folklore/Agricultural Museum** (1 June to 30 September, daily 4–6pm; tel: 22591, 22748). The marble plaque near the gate reads: 'Since the 16th century, the wind of Mykonos has turned the mill of (the) Boni (family)'. This is a beautiful vantage point, winter and summer, dawn past dusk. Pigeons flutter in the adjacent dovecote and light on the mill's shaggy roof. Below, in sunshine, the harbour is dazzling; mysterious, in heavy mist or rain. A tiny threshing floor rounds out this *al fresco* mu-

Map labels:

Grammata Cape
Vigles
Mirsini
Mirsini Bay
MORO ERGO
Aï Lias Anomeritis Cape
Fokos
Gialoudia
Evros Cape
MYKONOS
Mavrovouni
Vathia
Lagada
PROFITIS ILIAS
Moni Paleokastrou
ANOMERITIS
Ag. Lias
Ano Mera
Panagia Tourliani
Fragias
Kalafatis
Tigani
Mykobar
Goni Cape
Kalo Livadi
Loulos
Tarsana
Aghia Anna
Kalafatis Cape
Aghia Anna Beach
Dimasto
Kalo Livadi Bay
Kardamida
Mavrokefalos Cape
Aegean Sea

•••••• Itinerary 2
•••••• Itinerary 3 (by boat)

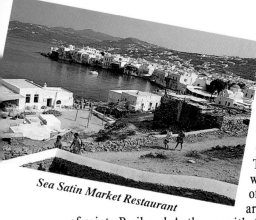

Sea Satin Market Restaurant

seum; those interested in a look within may return or take time out now.

Exit the red gate and turn left, proceeding downhill. Boni's windmill was the high point of this particular jaunt. Take note of Hora's dry stone walls, not as dramatic as those of Andros, but still a vanishing art form. Pass the twin chapels of saints Basil and Anthony, with their red roofs. Private villas crowd the road here and tiny gardens spill figs over their walls. In spring, almonds, and, later, children scaling the walls to plunder their nuts. The road plunges downwards, and a small olive grove on your left backs the Hotel Leto. Now, turn right on the Tourlos/San Stefanos road, and proceed for five minutes or so uphill, passing a large, circular threshing floor on your left. Very soon, also on your left, you will see a beautiful red-trimmed house incorporating a stunning 300-year-old dovecote into its roof, a fine example of Mykonos' vernacular architecture. Turn back at this point, unless you want to ramble a little further on the 'high' road to Tourlos, where refreshments are available.

Return to your turning off point on Aghiou Ioannou, where the Ano Mera/Elia beach/Tourlos/San Stefanos bus terminus is located, and bear right along the corniche. (This is the 'low' road to San Stefanos.) On your left, immediately, is the Remezzo Bar; below the wall around the curve in the road, the yacht basin and the pier where the ferries dock. On your right, a few metres on, is Mykonos' **Archaeological Museum** (open daily 8.30am–3pm, closed Monday).

This three-room building, usually deserted in the morning, is a little gem. Most striking of the holdings is a massive funeral amphora depicting the warrior-filled Trojan Horse and various gruesome scenes, in terracotta relief, from the Trojan War. Found in Hora, the vase dates from the 7th century BC. In the same

Awash in white

room are an assortment of the so-called 'Melian' vases, probably Parian in origin, all featuring the same sloe-eyed maiden in profile. In the south wing are funerary items from the Rheneian graves, including a whimsical satyr astride a phallus, of all things, and a lovely 'tigani' (literally 'frying pan') or water mirror, in whose liquid surface Cycladic ladies would have checked their make-up. Available for sale is a charming paper sculpture/toy for children based on the Trojan reliefs: a find at 800 drachmas.

After touring the museum, retrace your steps to the bus terminus-crossroads and turn left, down towards the harbour. On the corner here is the OTE building (telephone exchange), opposite several car-hire firms. The Hotel Leto, on your left, dates from 1953, and is one of the island's first. (The little beach on your right is not safe for bathing.) Entering Hora, tourist shops proliferate around the chapel of Aghia Anna (St Anne). Straight ahead is Lalaounis (see *Shopping*), but turn right towards the water now: at the end of this short street the columns date back 300 years and are made of Tiniot marble. In 1900, there were six. The charming, tiny Delos Hotel has been newly renovated.

Market fare

Turn left along the waterfront till you reach the bust of **Mando Mavrogennous** (see *History & Culture*), guarding Hora's main taxi square. The inscription translates roughly: 'Mando Mavrogennous, when her people needed her to secure their freedom, was given the title of protectress of the island.' To your right, along the harbourfront, you will see the **Sea & Sky Travel Agency**: go in and ask Takis Manesis for a map of Hora before heading back to Mando, where you will turn right and walk up Fl. Zouganeli Street. You will pass Andreas Pouloudis's bakery, a good place to pick up baked snacks of all sorts. Immediately on your right you will find Efthimios Efthimiou, a native Mykonian, whose **patisserie** has been operating for more than 15 years. Try his *kalathakia* (little almond cake 'baskets'), *amygthalotita* (almond biscuits), nougat, and macaroons. His boxed sweets make wonderful gifts, if you don't devour them before getting them home. (They are, however, very pricey!)

Exit Efthimiou's shop, and make a sharp left turning. Ahead of you is Kimon Koukouzelis's pharmacy (Monday to Saturday, 9am–1.30pm and 5–10.30pm, Sunday rotating hours shared with other pharmacies.) **Pierro's**, the long-infamous gay bar, is now on your left. Before the large church of Aghia Kyriaki, turn right for the International Press/Newsstand. Next door is a taverna called Kameni Gonia, the Burned Out Corner, named after a fire that gutted the place in 1976. Proceed down Kabani Street away from the church. At the first corner, turn left (do not proceed through the bougainvillaea-covered arch towards the port) and walk straight to Zannis Asimomitis's (John Silver-nose's) **grocery**, the least changed of all the island's *pandopoleia* (sellers-of-everything). Here, you will find incense and incense burners, rug beaters, rice and beans sold from sacks, Greek flags, beautiful Tiniot baskets, etc, etc.

As you exit from the store turn right and walk back down to Aghia Kyriaki; then turn right down Hora's main shopping street, **Matoyianni**. Amble along at your leisure, passing, on your left,

Asimomitis's grocery

the popular Anchor Bar and Ioannis Theoharis's pharmacy; on your right, Theodore Roussounellos's jewellery store. In addition to the National Bank of Greece and Commercial Bank branches on the harbour, you will find a Credit Bank on Matoyianni. Matoyianni turns right, becoming Enoplon Dinameon Street, at Vengera, a bar frequented by Athenian yuppiedom. Follow along Enoplon Dinameon, passing Lena's House Museum and the Aegean Maritime Museum. Just past the Maritime Museum, down an alleyway to your right, is the Sesame Kitchen (see *Eating Out*).

You are now entering the area of Hora called The Three Wells (*Tria Pigathia*), where there is a cluster of churches dedicated to saints George, Barbara and Fanourios, as well as the El Greco Restaurant and Astra Bar.

At the crossroads of Enoplon Dinameon and Mitropoleos streets is tiny **Mykonos Gold**, owned by Ioannis and Anna Michaelides. Tell Anna that Elizabeth sent you, and ask to see her seed-pearl and gold earrings, copies of 18th- and 19th-century heirlooms – the perfect gift for a bride-to-be, all hand-crafted by Ioannis and his sons. Again, take Mitropoleos Street to the right, a thoroughfare named for its Greek Orthodox and Roman Catholic cathedrals, at your own pace. About 400m (¼ mile) down the street, opposite Athanasios Kabana's sandal shop, are the cathedrals and, beyond them, the 'home' of Petros the Pelican II, Mykonos' mascot, in the area called **Alefkandra**. Detour here to peek inside the churches if you like; then return to Mitropoleos, passing, on your right, three churches, shoulder to shoulder: saints Nicholas (1616), Catherine and Paraskevi. Forge ahead on Mitropoleos towards the area called **Little Venice** and Kastro.

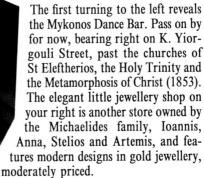

Petros II

The first turning to the left reveals the Mykonos Dance Bar. Pass on by for now, bearing right on K. Yiorgouli Street, past the churches of St Eleftherios, the Holy Trinity and the Metamorphosis of Christ (1853). The elegant little jewellery shop on your right is another store owned by the Michaelides family, Ioannis, Anna, Stelios and Artemis, and features modern designs in gold jewellery, moderately priced.

Opposite the Church of St John the Baptist, you will find fantastic T-shirt designs at Masakis. At the end of K. Yiorgoulis bear right downhill to one of the island's many good 'Nikos' tavernas for lunch. Nikos (Skepathianos) is noted for his fresh fish, but try his moussaka and a "roka" salad. Nikos also prepares authentic Greek sweets on the premises. Ask what's fresh today. Turn right out of Nikos's and head down to the waterfront again. Proceed right along the harbour, past the people-watchers in the expensive cafés, to the taxi square (remember Mando?). The little chapel you pass on your left, towards the sea, is sacred to St Nicholas, patron of sailors.

In the afternoon, you may want to catch a turquoise bus at the terminus just below the Maouna crossroads and ride out to Plati Yialos or Psarrou beaches for a swim. The buses are clearly marked, fares are reasonable, but expect passengers to be packed in like sardines in summer: fortunately, it's only 4km (2½ miles). **Plati Yialos** is a long, family orientated beach lined with tavernas and bars. **Psarrou** is a bit more exclusive. Jet skis and water sports are available on both beaches.

Little Venice

Moonlight over Mykonos

After catching a late bus back to town, call from your hotel to reserve a table at **Katrin's**, or just show up before 8pm at either the **Sesame Kitchen** or **La Bussola**, if you like Italian food (see *Eating Out*). In the morning, on your jaunt around and through Hora, you passed both the Mykonos Dance Bar and the Astra Bar. After dinner, and before it's jammed to the rafters, the **Mykonos Dance Bar** is the place to observe Greek dancing. **Astra** is more yuppified, with a sophisticated bar and dancing by a young, international set.

The nicest bar in town is the **Veranda** (or Green House), located in the Scarpa area, roughly between the Alefkandra and Kastro districts you traversed this morning. Head down Mitropoleos Street from the Mykonos Dance Bar and bear left along Ag. Anargiron Street; take the third narrow turning to the left. The Veranda is a gloriously restored 19th-century mansion overlooking the sea, with a view towards Delos (tel: 23719). It closes at 3.30am in high season – just a few hours before owner Ivan starts brewing espresso again at L'Angolo.

2. Ano Mera, Elia and Fresh Seafood

By hire car to the village of Ano Mera; visit the Monastery of the Panagia Tourliani; lunch at Maria Stavrakopoulou's taverna; drive to Elia beach for a swim; optional windsurfing at Kalafati Beach; dinner at O Vangelis.

Since, for this day-long itinerary, you will once again set out early in the morning from the Maouna crossroads, I suggest that you hire a car, preferably a covered jeep, from Mustang Rent A Car. (Call Damian Youlgaris or John Lerios from your hotel, and they'll arrange to deliver

Sun and sand

your vehicle directly to you; tel: 0289 22792/23143/24139.)

Head away from the crossroads in a northeasterly direction along Aghiou Ioannou Street, taking a hard right uphill after a short distance. This is the Ano Mera Village/Kalafatis beach road. You will be climbing steep switchbacks and passing a thatchless windmill; the Shell station on your left is one of three petrol stations on Mykonos (open daily 8am–7pm; weekends and holidays 8am–1pm); 200m (650ft) further on, also on the left, is the island's Health Centre. You will find a BP station about 1km (½ mile) further along.

You have now reached the barren high plateau of Mykonos, sparsely vegetated with thyme and oregano, studded by dusty rocks. For those with time for a 45-minute detour, there's a left turning half a kilometre past the BP station, poorly marked, for the as-yet-undeveloped northern beaches of Aghios Sostis and Panormos. These long expanses of virgin sand are beautiful and uncrowded, yet each boasts a good small taverna. En route to them, you will pass the mysterious, cross-studded Monastery of Aghios Pandeleimonos, with its walled garden. Bear right following signs for K.I. Sarandopoulos A.E., the future site of Mykonos's manmade reservoir. The **Panormos** beach turn-off, 1km (¾ mile) past the reservoir site, also leads to rooms for rent, should you decide to get away from it all. The beach is *laissez faire* as far as bathing costumes go. Andonis's taverna serves Greek fare and seafood, from Easter to October.

Approximately 2km (1¼ miles) beyond Panormos, after a climb and descent through lunar landscape, is the **Aghios Sostis** beach turn-off. The twin chapels here are thronged with celebrants on the feast day of St Sostis, 7 September – a wonderful time to visit this tiny community. Otherwise, Kiki's taverna offers sustenance for sun-dazzled bathers in summer.

Retrace your dusty tracks to the main Ano Mera road, and turn left. After 2km (1¼ miles), in the desolate epicentre of the island, is Mykonos's bizarre version of the

Monastery of the Panagia Tourliani

Hard Rock Cafe, aka the 'Acropolis of Rock'. Here, for the very young at heart, are nighttime fun and games in the form of video arcades, snooker/billiards tables, lots of spirit(s) and noise. On the left, a further 2km (1¼ miles), is the reliable Zygos taverna. Just beyond, as you enter the village of **Ano Mera**, bear right into town and find parking on the roundabout/town square. The village is the second largest settlement on Mykonos. Abutting the square is the long, low **Monastery of Panagia Tourliani**, sacred to the Virgin, whose feast day falls on 15 August. Founded in 1767, the monastery is open daily 10am–1pm. In modest dress, do peek inside the church and ask Bishop Filaretos or Father-Monk Theologos for a tour of the little folk museum, housed in the monastery's 19th-century bakery. A still for *raki*, the Greek version of moonshine (or the Turkish ouzo), figures prominently here.

Afterwards, retire to the Stavrakopoulos family's café/taverna, **O Vangelis** (tel: 0289 71577), for lunch, sheltering under shady eucalyptus trees on the square. Here I recommend you order the massive Greek salad, grilled octopus or whitebait, and Mykonos's trademark cheese, *kopanisti*, from my old friends, Maria, her son Stavros, and her daughters and daughter-in-law.

Mykonos farmhouse

After lunch, and perhaps a coffee and Greek sweet – you could try *galaktoboureko* or *kadaïfi* – at daughter Irini's sweet shop, just across the square (tel: 0289 71144), ask to be pointed in the direction of Elia beach and exit the square in an easterly direction. Signs for Elia clearly mark your route.

Proceed about 1km (½ mile) and take a sharp right at the football pitch. In your descent to the sea you will pass low whitewashed farmhouses and gardens kept alive through sheer determination. **Elia**, reached after a further kilometre (½ mile), is a developed sandy beach (the longest on Mykonos) with umbrellas, lounge chairs, good tavernas and clear blue water. It's a popular nudist beach, too, and can get very busy in high season.

Windsurfing aficionados may want to give Elia a miss and turn left instead of right at the football pitch. This is the Kalafatis beach road. After approximately 3km (1¾ miles), you will see to your right the twin peaks of Cape Kalafatis. Follow signs for the Paradise Aphrodite Beach Hotel, but stop short of the hotel itself at Kalafati Beach. Here are the beach umbrellas and colourful surf gear of the **Happy Surfpool Centre**, German-run and open from 1 May to mid-October. (Anyone especially interested in wind-surfing should ask for a brochure detailing other Surfpool Centres in the Cyclades, notably on Paros and Santorini.)

After a relaxing afternoon spent swimming or surfing, return to Ano Mera for dinner, perhaps fish of the day caught by Anna's son, Kyriakos.

3. Southern Beaches

On foot or by bus to Plati Yialos beach; a hike from beach to cove to beach along the southern coast; stop at Coco Club on Super Paradise beach for a good lunch, or proceed to Elia beach.

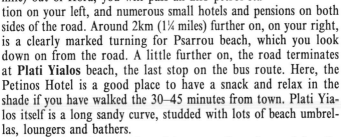

Once again, your starting point is Maouna, at the crossroads, if you are travelling by hire car or on foot. Set out from here in a southerly direction on the Plati Yialos road. If you prefer to use public transport, head downhill to the Plati Yialos/Psarrou/Paradise bus terminus. A little over 1km (½ mile) out of Hora, you will pass an EKO petrol station on your left, and numerous small hotels and pensions on both sides of the road. Around 2km (1¼ miles) further on, on your right, is a clearly marked turning for Psarrou beach, which you look down on from the road. A little further on, the road terminates at **Plati Yialos** beach, the last stop on the bus route. Here, the Petinos Hotel is a good place to have a snack and relax in the shade if you have walked the 30–45 minutes from town. Plati Yialos itself is a long sandy curve, studded with lots of beach umbrellas, loungers and bathers.

The pier here is the point of departure for caiques plying the southern coast. The fares are reasonable, and it's a pleasant way to commute to nudist beaches up the coast, or even around the bluff to Psarrou. (Mykonos Boat Trips manager Anthony Theoharis, tel: 23995, can also arrange day-long caique trips for private parties, and show you more secluded coves up this sunny coast.) Ten minutes away are the Aghia Anna and Paranga beaches, reached by caique. Nikola's taverna at **Aghia Anna** is a gem of a Greek bistro and a great place for breakfast, lunch or dinner, Easter to 20 October. Fifteen minutes from Plati Yialos, by caique, is **Paradise**, a nudist beach-cum-campsite that appeals to the college-age

Plati Yialos

Fisherman's caique

set. Five minutes further on is **Super Paradise**, a gorgeous, tiny cove which features the excellent if pricey Coco Bar restaurant. Another five minutes by boat brings you to **Agrari**; **Elia**, the end of the boat line, is yet another five-minute chug. The caique trip in itself is an indelible Mykonian experience. From 20 April until mid-October, this is a great way to tour the beaches and get a taste of the fishermen's life: your stalwart boatmen fish for a living and ferrying tourists is their seasonal sideline.

For those who arrive off-season or who prefer to walk, it's a 30-minute hike to Paranga. Cut across Plati Yialos, away from the Hotel Petinos, and head up into the rocks at the end of the beach. The dirt track above the sea is well worn. Bear right, following painted signs for Paranga/Paradise. After passing two stone stiles, you will come to (yet another) chapel dedicated to St Anne. The tiny beach here is Aghia Anna, and Costas and Anna, of course, are ready to welcome you with cold beer at Nikola's taverna. **Paranga**, a larger beach, is just further south, but the hideous Camping Mykonos will discourage hikers from proceeding on to Paradise. Until very recently, this corniche for walkers was mostly free of development. Now, this campsite resembling a 1990s concentration camp has obliterated the stark natural beauty beyond Paranga. At Nikola's, however, such eyesores are out of sight and mind.

4. Evening Museums and Paraportiani

Folklore Museum; Paraportiani Church; Aegean Maritime Museum; Lena's House Museum.

Your starting point, at about 5.30pm, is the little blue-domed chapel of St Nicholas on the waterfront in **Hora**. Proceed in a westerly direction towards the pier where the boats for Delos (*MV Hera*, etc) dock, and set off up a flight of steps where a small sign points the way to the windmills, Little Venice and Paraportiani Church. Several metres on, you will see Mykonos's **Folklore Museum** on your right, a complex of white buildings with crimson doors and shutters (daily, in summer, 5.30–8.30pm; tel: 22591), and the elegant, sphinx-like Church of Paraportiani a bit further on, located on your left.

This is the **Kastro district** of Hora, the original, fortified medieval city, but the Folklore Museum preserves the heritage of a more recent culture: Mykonos of the 18th and 19th centuries, in its heyday as a naval power. As you enter, look up to your left: this museum is the final resting place of the original Petros the Pelican, immortalised by taxidermy. There are several important permanent exhibits here, notably commemorative china plates, tools of measurement, relief carvings in marble, and nine elaborate rosewood and gilt Venetian *scrinios*, massive chests/secretaires. The Venetian photogravure collection dates from the early 20th century. Votive offerings are displayed in a revolving case, idiosyncratic 'prayers' in gold, silver or tin, offered up by the afflicted to preserve or heal a marriage, an eye, a leg, a horse, etc. Within the museum, as well, is a complete Mykonian residence, preserved as it was in 1864, complete with kitchen. In the basement, another collection mirrors Mykonos's nautical history. Here are a customised model of a Mykonian caique, and a replica of an 1821 warship's deck, incorporating original elements such as cannon, perhaps those fired by Mando Mavrogennous.

Exiting the Folklore Museum, proceed on to view the **Church of Our Lady Paraportiani**, actually a cluster of chapels dedicated to the Virgin, the Aghii Anargyri (the 'Penniless Saints', Cosmas and Damian), St Anastasia, St Sostis and St Efstathios, parts of which may date back to the 15th century. Paraportiani, best viewed at sunset against the rosy summer sky, is surely one of the world's most beautiful man-made structures, an enigma of light and line that has long fascinated visitors and artists.

Circling the assymetrical church, you will pass the Kastro Bar on your right, a wonderful place to watch the sunset, view an exhibition by a local painter, and enjoy the music. This evening, however, there are two more museums which are worth seeing, so proceed

down Aghion Anargiron Street through the Kastro district. Several metres further along is the Montparnasse Bar, a Mykonos landmark, also on your right, with a lovely view to the sea, temporary exhibitions of local artists' work, classical music and an élite clientele. At the next corner, look right to the sea: here is the Veranda (Green House) bar, for future reference. At a narrow crossroads, Aghion Anargiron and Mitropoleos streets converge. Go straight on along Mitropoleos, passing Anna Gelou's snowy

Paraportiani church

White Shop on your right, festooned with lace and white pullovers. Forge on, passing the cathedrals on your right. On a busy evening, you may find yourself shouldering your way through crowds for 20 minutes or so before reaching the end of Mitropoleos. Here, turn left into Enoplon Dinameon Street. Another few metres, past a kiosk on your left, you will enter the Three Wells district, pass El Greco Restaurant (where the three wells themselves separate diners from dancers at the Astra Bar).

To the left, past the Church of St George, is The Sesame Kitchen restaurant, down a tiny alley. On Enoplon Dinameon, at No 10, with a cannon out front, is your next destination, the **Aegean Maritime Museum** (daily, in summer, 10.30am–1pm and 6.30–9pm). Curator Philip Menardos, a tenth-generation Mykonian, will show you around the museum, housed in the former manse of Revolutionary War hero Captain Nikolas Sourmelis, who aided the Cretan insurgents in 1866. The various permanent exhibits here detail 'the Greekness of the Aegean, from antiquity through to the present,' says Menardos. Models of ships predominate, including a replica of Sourmelis's *Enosis*, but there are also nautical instruments, coins, maps, paintings and photographs, ships' logs and books. The first registry book of Modern Greece, dating from 1871, is housed here. In the garden stands the lighthouse which dominated Hora's pier from 1890 till 1983.

Adjacent to the Maritime Museum is **Lena's House**, at No 8 Enoplon Dinameon, a typical 19th-century Mykonian burgher's house, from hardwood floors to rafters (Monday to Saturday 6–9pm, Sunday 7–9pm). Donated to Mykonos's Folklore Museum in 1970 by the Dracopoulos family, the house catches in amber a vanished culture. Lena Scrivanou, the maiden lady whose home this was, maintained it much as her grandmother had left it. The furnishings, ferried home by Mykonian sea captains, hail from northern Europe. The photogravures illustrate scenes from Homer. Lena's lace-making apparatus and iron Austrian bed, decorated with cameo portraits, her needlework and boxed chamber pot, all comprise an integrated whole. After being shown round by Mrs Margarita Xythaki, you are on your own for the evening, to dine in the Three Wells area or shop your way down Matoyianni Street.

Evening visit to 'fauve' painters Luis Orozco's and Dorlies Schapitz's gallery and studio.

In the 1960s, when I first visited Mykonos, the Cyclades were a magnet for painters from the Americas and Northern Europe. Many arrived as tourists and, beguiled by Cycladic architecture and the light and colour of Greece, stayed on. Luis Orozco was one such artist. Since 1960, he has maintained a studio on the island, and opened, as well, Mykonos's first art gallery.

In recent years, Orozco has shared his life, and gallery space, with former pupil, Dorlies Schapitz. Their oils are variations on a theme: bold landscapes, still lifes and portraits which capture fully the island's dramatic palette. Luis and Dorlies live in the Fournakia quarter of Hora, so give them a call at their studio (tel: 24016) or at the Orama Gallery (tel: 26339) and arrange to meet them and see their paintings. Orama is located several metres from Mykonos's Aegean Maritime Museum and Lena's House, on a sidestreet off Enopleon Dinameon Street.

Luis, born in Mexico City, has exhibited all over the United States, throughout northern Europe and Greece. His paintings hang in the Montparnasse Piano Bar and El Greco Restaurant on Mykonos. Dorlies, born in Rehsen, Germany, also exhibits locally. Both artists have permanent exhibitions in Santa Fe, New Mexico. The couple are in residence on Mykonos, and hard at work painting, from early spring through October, and then spend the winter in Europe and the Americas, exhibiting.

After visiting their gallery, you may want to see Luis's and Dorlies's studio: feel free to ask them. (Luis is an accomplished portraitist. If you are inclined to sit, you might want to have a look at his archive of portraits past.)

Round off your evening of art with a late drink at the Montparnasse Piano

Luis Orozco

Work by Dorlies Schapitz

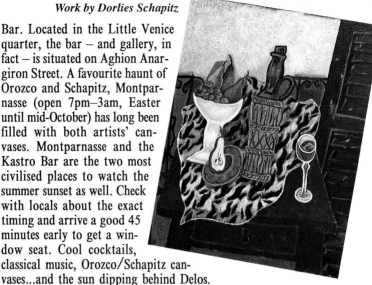

Bar. Located in the Little Venice quarter, the bar – and gallery, in fact – is situated on Aghion Anargiron Street. A favourite haunt of Orozco and Schapitz, Montparnasse (open 7pm–3am, Easter until mid-October) has long been filled with both artists' canvases. Montparnasse and the Kastro Bar are the two most civilised places to watch the summer sunset as well. Check with locals about the exact timing and arrive a good 45 minutes early to get a window seat. Cool cocktails, classical music, Orozco/Schapitz canvases...and the sun dipping behind Delos.

6. Private Tour of the Holy Isle of Delos

By 9.45am boat to Delos; privately guided tour of the archaeological site and museum; return to Mykonos at 2pm.

This is a relatively expensive tour of Apollo's sacred isle but, in this author's estimation, one of the most remarkable daytrips in the Mediterranean, and worth every drachma. Call your guide, Aleka Angeletaki (tel: 22537), to arrange your tour and enquire about her fee a night or two before you plan to go. Do remember, both Delos's site and museum close on Monday. (I suggest you pick up a copy of Aleka's godmother's book, *Delos: Monuments and Museums*, by Photini Zaphiropoulou, on Mykonos, and read up beforehand.) Have an early breakfast at one of Hora's harbourfront cafés near the chapel of St Nicholas, and meet Aleka at the head of the pier where the Delos boats dock, at the time she suggests. The large, stable *MV Hera* (fare, 1,500 drachmas, round trip) takes around 30 minutes to make the crossing, which can be rough in windy weather. Be sure to bring a jacket.

Delos, which resembles nothing so much as a huge *al fresco* museum of marble rubble, punctuated by more explicable treasures such as the Avenue of the Naxian Lions and the mosaic floors, is confusing to visitors. Delos's demise is a story in itself. During the Hellenistic era, the Syrian king of Pontus, Mithridates, destroyed the island in 88BC in the course of his war with Rome. He razed Delos, sacked the rich treasuries, and killed some 20,000 people, sparing the valuable slaves. The Romans then fortified the city and sanctuary, but the pirate Athenodoros, Mithridates's ally, returned for the kill and dealt Delos its death blow in 69BC.

Aleka's guided tour is arranged chronologically, to help you better appreciate the holy isle's long, complex history. (A licensed archaeological guide, Aleka is one of only five on Mykonos legally entitled to escort visitors to Delos.)

Immediately after docking at the new pier on the west side of the islet, proceed through a gate (fee 1,000 drachmas; Sunday free) and go straight on. Delos has been inhabited since the 3rd millennium BC, when the pre-Hellenic Carians settled Mt Kynthos, on protected high ground. Later, in the 2nd millennium, they descended to the plain when Delos became a Minoan port. Then came the Ionians, who initiated the cult of Apollo, said to have been born on Delos along with his twin sister, Artemis, goddess of the hunt, and chastity. The cult is now dated at around the 8th–7th century BC.

Aleka will first guide you through the **Sanctuary of Apollo**, clearly delineated by schist walls. By the 3rd–2nd century BC this area was chock-a-block with monuments erected by special interest groups and it was necessary to add extensions to house the overflowing collection of statuary and relics. Two Hellenistic dynasties, of Philip V and of Pergamon, funded these marble structures as a sort of self-advertisement. (A model of the buildings in the museum helps you visualise the architectural complexity of this area.)

Aleka will then point out the road connecting Delos's ancient port with the sanctuary, a late addition to the site and in use since the 7th century BC, and the 2nd-century BC steps marking the entrance to the temple. A Hermaic stele still guards the steps. Here the Ionian celebrants arrived bearing gifts for the god. The procession, led by priests of Apollo, made its way to the altar to sacrifice animals, primarily bulls. The Apollonian festivals, called the Delia, after Delos, occurred annually for some eight centuries, but individuals might come to Delos (the Lourdes of antiquity) at any time during the year to ask Apollo for special favours.

Avenue of the Naxian Lions

To the right, inside the sanctuary, is a massive marble base. The Naxians, most powerful in the region in the 7th century BC, here erected a 7-m (22-ft) tall marble statue of a wasp-waisted Apollo, which broke above its bronze belt in an earthquake. Beside the statue is the **House of the Naxians**, who were Delos's first governors. (Ask Aleka to tell you about the procedure for constructing those massive Naxian sculptures, some of which you can still see *in situ* on Naxos itself.)

Further on are the **three temples** dedicated to Apollo, the first dating from 540BC, when the 'purification' of Delos was carried out by the Athenian tyrant Peiseistratos, who removed all graves from the sanctuary. The second temple, of the Athenians, dates from the classical era and that of the Delian League. Temples were used to store and safeguard wealth, like banks, and to house the valuable statues of the god. It was in the 5th century BC that the second 'purification' of Delos was enacted — literally carried out to oust the native Delians from their homeland. After a brief Athenian ascendancy, Delos fell under the influence of the Macedonian dynasty of Philip II, father of Alexander the Great. The Delians themselves completed the third temple to Apollo during this period of relative independence for the island.

On to the **Temple of Artemis**, part of which dates from 2000BC, as evidenced by ivory artefacts now in the museum. This structure was always dedicated to a goddess, whether this was Artemis or some unknown predecessor. Up the hill stand the ruins of five treasuries dating from various periods, indicative of the degeneration of Delos as a place of purely religious pilgrimage and its gradual metamorphosis into a sort of huge Cycladic bank vault.

Beyond the treasuries is the **Temple of Leto**, mother of the Olympian twins, the sacred lake where Apollo and Artemis were said to have been born, and the **Avenue of the Naxian Lions**. This area became progressively more crowded with shops and restaurants during the Hellenistic era, when Delos was as busy as Mykonos in August. Down a long street of Hellenistic workshops is the Minoan Fountain, once covered and used as a source of drinking water: the phallic statuary here was sacred to Dionysos. On a gentle rise is a **snack bar** — a pleasant place for a rest and refreshment — and the **Archaeological Museum**, which contains objects of art from the various private Hellenistic villas, erected when the island's population of freemen numbered some 25,000. In the collection are also the first examples of individualised portrait statues, idealised archaic *kouroi*, in addition to classical statuary.

About 1km (½ mile) south of the museum are the shops of the Hellenistic era, restaurants and private mansions. The **House of Dionysos**, named after its mosaic of the god astride a tiger (this minutely rendered mosaic utilises 29 tiles for the pupil of the tiger's eye alone) is a multi-storeyed dwelling which belonged to a merchant. Don't be misled by the white marble here – the interior was once a riot of colour, walls, columns, etc, all painted garishly.

Nearby, **Cleopatra's House** was inhabited by a (not *the*) Cleopatra and her husband Dioskourides, most probably suburban Athenians, who came to Delos in 138BC. Their portrait statues still stand in the house, erected by Cleopatra herself in honour of her spouse, obviously a way for a nouveau riche couple to display their considerable wealth. Beyond the residential quarter is the theatre, built in 300BC, which Aleka calls 'a piece of work' – an understatement. It was not constructed within a natural amphitheatre, and yet seated 5,500, an architectural feat of some importance at that time. Another surprise: the theatre doubled as a reservoir. It was used to channel rainwater into a giant underground cistern.

Aleka ends your tour with two houses containing Delos's most striking mosaics, the dolphins and, in the House of the Masks, the mosaic of Dionysos, god (also) of the theatre, riding a panther. If you have time left after viewing the mosaics, ask to see the sanctuary of the foreign gods – Egyptian and Syrian deities such as Isis, Sarapis, Adat and Atargati.

Visitors for whom one visit to Delos is not enough may ask Aleka to return on subsequent days. Realistically speaking, it takes about four days to view all the important aspects of the island site.

House of Cleopatra

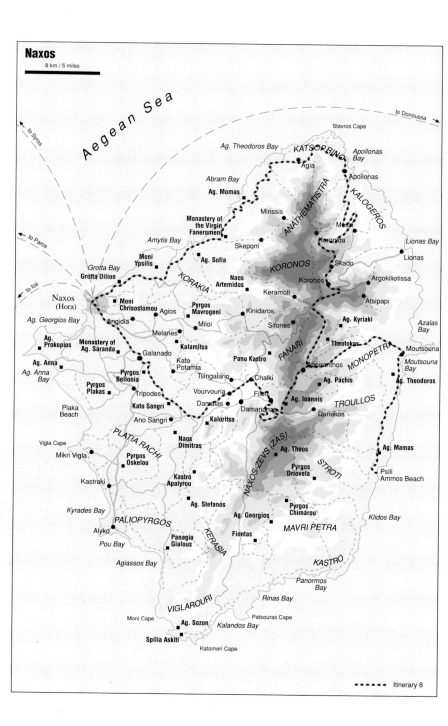

Naxos

8 km / 5 miles

Aegean Sea

to Donoussa

to Syros

to Paros

to Ios

Stavros Cape

Ag. Theodoros Bay

KATSOPRINO

Agia

Apollonas Bay

Apollonas

Abram Bay

Ag. Momas

Mirissis

ANATHEMATISTRA

KALOGEROS

Messi

Monastery of the Virgin Faneromeni

Skeponi

Koronida

Lionas Bay

Amytis Bay

KORONOS

Skado

Lionas

Moni Ypsilis

Ag. Sofia

Koronos

Argokiliotissa

Grotta Bay
Grotta Dilion

KORAKIA

Naos Artemidos

Keramoti

Atsipapi

Azalas Bay

Naxos (Hora)

Moni Chrisostomou

Agios

Pyrgos Mavrogeni

Kinidaros

Ag. Kyriaki

Ag. Georgios Bay

Angidia

Miloi

Sifones

FANARI

Theotokos

MONOPETRA

Moutsouna

Ag. Prokopios

Monastery of Ag. Saranda

Melanes

Kalamitsa

Pano Kastro

Apeiranthos

Moutsouna Bay

Galanado

Kato Potamia

Tsingalario

Ag. Pachis

Ag. Theodoros

Ag. Anna

Ag. Anna Bay

Pyrgos Bellonia

Chalki

Ag. Ioannis

TROULLOS

Pyrgos Plakas

Tripodes

Vourvouria

Filoti

Danakos

Kato Sangri

Damalas

Damarionas

Plaka Beach

Ano Sangri

Kaloritsa

NAXOS-ZEVS (ZAS)

Ag. Mamas

Vigla Cape

PLATIA RACHI

Naos Dimitras

Ag. Theos

STROTI

Psili Ammos Beach

Mikri Vigla

Pyrgos Oskelou

Pyrgos Driovela

Kastraki

Kastro Apalyrou

Klidos Bay

Kyrades Bay

PALIOPYRGOS

Ag. Stefanos

Ag. Georgios

Pyrgos Chimárou

MAVRI PETRA

Alyko

Panagia Gialous

KERASIA

Fiontas

Pou Bay

Agiassos Bay

KASTRO

Panormos Bay

Rinas Bay

VIGLAROURI

Moni Cape

Ag. Sozon

Patsouras Cape

Kalandos Bay

Spilia Askiti

Katomeri Cape

•••••• Itinerary 8

40

Naxos

In summer, it is advisable to book your ferry (catamaran or hydrofoil) tickets, and to reserve accommodation well in advance. If you are leaving Mykonos for Naxos (or other Cycladic islands) see Mr Takis Manesis at Sea & Sky Travel in Hora beforehand to discuss sea connections and fax ahead to your next destination for accommodation. The crossing time to Naxos varies, according to which ship you take. Note that catamarans and hydrofoils operate during summer, but not in foul weather. Plan to leave Hora, Mykonos at about 9am and reach Naxos's capital city and main port, also called Hora, by midday. Two of the hotels recommended in *Practical Information* are located in the Kastro quarter of Hora: you have a hike up from the port upon disembarkation, but the quiet and the view will reward your efforts.

Naxos Tourist Information Centre is on the harbourfront in Hora, across from the bus terminus. Kostas and Despina Kitini will arrange island tours, connections and accommodation. If you are staying at their Hotel Zevgoli, drop your luggage here for transport uphill. (Tel: 0285 25200, fax: 0285 24358. In Athens, tel: 01-651 5885.)

The Passenger Tourist & Travel Office is also on the harbourfront: be on the lookout for distinctive red and blue flags out front. Captain Michaeli Dendrinos arranges all sea connections. (Tel: 0285 24581/22715, fax: 0285 24581.)

Hora, Naxos

A full day. Breakfast or lunch at the Meltemi; stroll to the Portara; walking tour of the Old Agora quarter; the Kastro quarter; the Tower of Crispi; Palace of Marco Sanudo; Catholic Cathedral; Jesuit School where Nikos Kazantzakis studied; the Archaeological Museum.

If you arrive from Mykonos on the *Paros Express* or the hydrofoil, and haven't had much to eat, head down the harbour from the northern pier to the **Meltemi Restaurant**, and have breakfast or lunch outside by the water. After noon, try their fresh grilled fish or traditional Greek dishes such as *pastitsio* (Greek lasagna) or *yemistes* (stuffed peppers, courgettes or tomatoes). Your point of departure for this walking tour of Hora is the massive **Portara** (huge portal) on the spit of land lying to the extreme north of the harbour town.

It's an easy climb, except on the hottest of days, and affords a dramatic view of Naxos's busy capital. **Hora** has been continuously inhabited for five millennia, making it one of Greece's oldest towns. Once an islet, the promontory where the massive doorway stands is the spot where the ancients believed Ariadne, daughter of the mythical King Minos of Crete, was rescued by the Olympian winegod, Dionysos, claimed by the Naxians as a native, if immortal, son. The tripartite entrance (Portara) is all that remains of an Ionian temple to Apollo, begun by the tyrant Lygdamis in 530BC. The Naxians liked to do things in a big way, as evidenced by the colossal *kouroi*, archaic statues of young men or gods, abandoned unfinished in marble quarries above the villages of Apollonas and Flerio, as well as the giant Apollo erected by the Naxians on Delos. But the Portara, made of only three gigantic stones, is perhaps most impressive, framing nothing but the Mediterranean sky. Looking out on Naxos's Hora, you can see the boomerang sweep of the harbourfront, with its string of shish kebab and souvenir shops. But rising above the concrete cubes of the 1960s and 1970s is the Kastro quarter, the fortified-city-above-the-Greek-city first erected by the Venetians.

To orientate yourself, look down from the Portara to the left. Behind the Elli Restaurant and back is the Grotta district. The **Plateia**, or main square, area centres on the wide, open space on the harbour where the turquoise island buses originate and the tamarisk-shaded park where the bronze statue of Petros Protopapadakis stands. (The village of Apeiranthos has produced many illustrious scholars and

The Portara

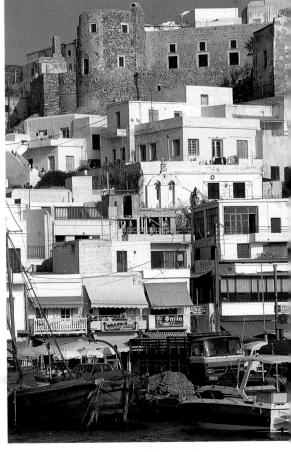

statesmen. Protopapad-
akis, once Minister of
Finance, was credited
with and executed for
the disastrous rout of
Greek troops in the
Asia Minor Campaign
but he's still revered
here at home.) The
Bourgo, or Old Agora
quarter, a maze of resi-
dential alleyways loca-
ted off the Plateia,
reflects 13th-century
Venetian influences.
But, above the Bourgo,
Kastro is the cre-
nellated crown of the
whole town.

Heading downhill
from the Portara now,
cross the causeway
again. To your left,
hugging the moun-
tains, is the **Monastery
of St John the Golden-
mouthed**, whose feast
day is 13 November. To your right stretches many-peaked Paros.
Next to the Bus Organization Office, about 10m (32ft) further on
is the Catholic Church of Saint Anthony (summer mass, 7pm), across
the street from the bus depot for village buses. The obelisk, with a
relief of a mourning Pallas Athena, is a memorial to Naxos's fallen
soldiers, 1897–1922. Pass Nicholas Dellaroka's chemist's shop on
your right (9am–1.30pm and 5–10.30pm) and, on your left, dwarfed
in mid-harbour, the tiny chapel of the Virgin of Myrtle, erected in
1707, once part of the Venetian dock but now an islet.

Exactly opposite the Myrditiotissa Chapel is a small square surrounded by cafés, with a kiosk on the curb and, on one corner, a
massive gift shop/liquor store called Probonas, which sells quality
Naxian specialities such as citron liqueur. Turn uphill here and
proceed up Ag. Nikodemus Street, named after Naxos's native-born
patron saint (feast day, 14 July). Pass under an arch and bear right
up Apollonas Street, following signs for the Archaeological Museum.
You are now in the **Bourgo**, or **Old Agora** district.

Ten metres (32ft) up this winding alley on your right is a shop
called The Loom, which sells Greek antiques, hand-woven clothing
and fabrics and other so-called 'Popular Greek Arts' – a good place
to browse. (Don't miss the shadow puppets, sheep's bells and worked
silver belt buckles.) Continuing on, you come to a T-junction where

geraniums spill down a wall. Turn right. Proceed another ten metres and reach a marble portal, called Porta tou Yalou, the first of five Venetian check-points travellers had to pass – showing their documents, a sort of passport – in order to reach the medieval stronghold of **Kastro**. Outside this first portal, on the left behind a blue door, is the Church of the Prophet Elijah. Retrace your steps now to the T-junction.

To your left, through an archway, was located the Greek Orthodox enclave of Bourgo, outside the Catholic Kastro. Notice, at this crossroads, the characteristic, rounded corners on the dwellings: these were designed to protect the walls from damage by heavily laden pack animals. Turn right up the steps here, leaving the Bourgo below you: 20m (64ft) up, pass through another archway – a wrought-iron circular stair on your left – and turn left. Turn right, following Archaeological Museum signs. Here begin the walls of the Kastro quarter, erected by Marco Sanudo's Venetian dynasty beginning in 1207, when the Venetian adventurer seized 17 Aegean islands. Rising on your left is the **Tower of Crispi**, the sole remaining rampart of a dozen former watchtowers. The Kastro seems an unwalled citadel today, because the inhabitants of Hora, who moved in after the fall of the Venetians, cleverly made houses of the castle's fortifications.

Ahead of you now is the last of the portals that medieval Naxians had to clear on their way up, the Trani Porta. Locals claim the wooden door is 700 years old. Five metres (16ft) on, turn left, again following museum signs. The Kastro is a citadel of houses, whose outer walls once formed a keep, as is apparent here. The outer walls are 1½m (5ft) thick at the top and close to 2½m (8ft) thick at the base. Directly after passing through the Trani Porta, the Large Gate, turn left up M. Sanudos Street (following museum signs), and look back. Above the arch is a house with a heraldic shield over the door: Duke Crispi's escutcheon.

Here, ignore the yellow museum signs and go straight on. If you're fortunate, you'll see into one of the houses here, where gardens back street-side doors. Note the windows: the panes on the outside; shutters inside – to keep out the cold, it's believed. All the rooftops in Kastro once joined, to enable the locals' easier escape from marauding pirates. Some 30m (96ft) on, M. Sanudos Street opens onto a small square with a tree in the centre. Here is the Catholic boarding school of St Anthony, which still houses some students in summer, though the numbers of Cycladic Catholics

Island pastime

have dwindled dramatically. Turn right out of the square and go up-hill: take the first left turning. Bear right out onto a crenellated terrace. Below you to the left is yet another of the formerly locked gates into Kastro, now gone: only the steps remain. Before you stretches the new city and the **Church of St Kyriaki**, once a monastery (feast day, 7 July). All the buildings behind this church date from the 20th century. To the left, on a hill now covered with houses, is a memorial to the Greek Sacred Squadron, which helped liberate the islands from the Germans in World War II: these soldiers were called the Angels of the Aegean, and are still talked about with reverence. (Naxos was liberated on 15 October 1944, three days after Athens.)

Retrace your steps to St Anthony's Square, and turn left up M. Sanudos Street under the arch. Take the first left – 5m (16ft) past the arch – up two steps into a small alley. Wind up and up, in single file. A small church on your left is the Greek Orthodox Church of the God-covered Virgin. This was once the sole Greek Orthodox church within the Kastro and antedated Venetian Sanudo: he was crowned Duke of Naxos here. Adjacent was the Palace of Marco Sanudo, now the residence of the Catholic bishop.

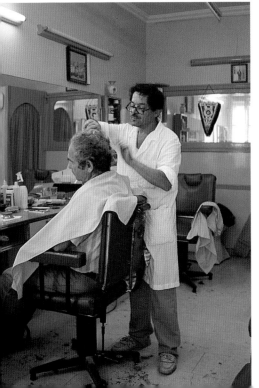

On your right is the back of the **Catholic Cathedral** (feast day, 2 February). The little square here is the epicentre of the Kastro. Here, the massive stone wall – the Main Tower, only the lower portion of which has survived – contains marble blocks taken from the Portara, and it was here that the island's original human settlement was located. Turn right downhill from here into another small square with a tree. The Cathedral here celebrates mass on Sunday at 9.30am; daily, 5.30pm. Herein are two special icons: a double-

A snip at the price

sided representation of the Virgin standing and St John – rare because the Virgin holds Christ, uncharacteristically, on her right arm. The second icon dates from the 12th century and depicts the Virgin nursing the Infant. Retrace your steps from the Cathedral to the stone wall and turn up past the ducal palace. Follow signs for the Archaeological Museum, housed in the former Jesuit Commercial School, where novelist Nikos Kazantzakis studied.

Naxos's **Archaeological Museum** (daily 8.30am–3pm, closed Sunday, Monday and holidays, entrance free) contains the most diverse and complete collection of Cycladic artefacts in the world. The finds from the 3rd millennium BC and the later Late Mycenaean holdings are unique and merit some study. Purchase the guidebook to the collection at the door and seek out the 50-cm (19-inch) tall Keros idol, the small pregnant Naxian idol and, a rarity, the male idol. There is a significant collection of jars, or *hydria*, one with dancers linked, hand to hand, resembling the dancing Greeks of today. Another vessel depicts fishermen netting tuna. The most beautiful object in the museum is a 6th-century BC **marble head** of a *kouros*, or idealised youth.

Mikri Vigla beach

Turn left after exiting the museum, passing under the statue of the Virgin in the Ursuline Convent's flyover. Proceed down a gentle flight of steps. On your left, you pass the Dellaroca mansion, its marble heraldic shield above a dark blue door. Follow the path downhill, bearing left through two stone arches, and ending up in a square graced by an excellent restaurant, **To Kastro Taverna** (see *Eating Out*), and the marble bust of a Macedonian hero, Christos Pradounas, for whom this square is named. Pass To Kastro and head downhill under three arches, passing the **Oniro Roof Garden Restaurant** on the way. Take the first right downhill. Turn left in front of a small church and go straight on. Roll straight downhill to reach the port: any path will do.

In the afternoon, you may want to board a bus from Hora for one of the west-coast beaches: **Aghios Georgios**, with its windsurfing facilities; **Plaka**, and dramatic **Mikri Vigla**, which also offers surfers' delights; or lovely, white **Alyko** or **Agiasos**. All these beaches are crowded in high season. (If you want to escape the hordes, head east.)

8. Hill Villages, Eastern Beaches and Apollonas

A full day's drive into the interior, taking in Chalki's Church of the Virgin; lunch in Filoti; Apeiranthos's museum; down to Moutsouna and the east coast beaches, or alternatively north to the gigantic statue of Apollonas, and west back to Hora.

After breakfast at your hotel or, preferably, at one of the harbourfront cafés, walk down to the southern end of the port and up the street that is a continuation of the **paraleia**, or waterfront promenade. Hire a car at Koufopoulos Rent A Car, and retrace your route to the corner (where the National Bank of Greece stands). Turn right and proceed 2km (1¼ miles) to the Elinoil Station to top up your tank. This is the main road to the hill villages of Chalki, Filoti and Apeiranthos, and to the northern port of Apollonas, your destinations today. (By the way, it will cost almost the amount of your car hire to fill your tank, so take this into account when deciding how much cash to carry.) After another 300m (1,000ft), you will reach the crossroads for Melanes (where, at Flerio, an ancient quarry contains a 7th-century-BC *kouros* 6½m/20ft long) and Sangri. Bear right. You are crossing the Plain of Livadi now, farm country, and your route is lined with lush vegetation, stands of reeds, and the sentinel-like agave trees, or 'Century Plants', a New World transplant.

Around 2km (1¼ miles) further on, you will reach another crossroads where the right hand route leads off to Tripodes and Ano Sangri. Bear left following the Koronos sign, and you will begin to climb. To your left, in the distance, is Hora, with Kastro crowning it. Northwards is the summit of Mt Koronas (997m/3,270ft). The first little village you will pass through, 5km (3 miles) out of Hora, is Galanado, red and green with hibiscus, but unprepossessing. Two kilometers further on, across from the Heracles cement

View of Naxos from the hills

Feeding time

works, the view of the island of Paros, and Kastro on a clear day is impressive. Over a pass, 1½km (1 mile) further, and Naxos's mountainous moonscape opens up before you, clouds and white Aegean light dappling putty-coloured peaks and crags. Ruined windmills on your right, and a derelict monastery 4½km (3 miles) further on mark a bad road to the west coast beach of Agiasos, but it's better to visit the beach another time via the road out of Hora. For the next 4km (2½ miles), olive groves proliferate and swallows and birds of prey crowd the sky. At 15km (9 miles) is a turn-off for the villages of Fouria and Damarianos. The Church of St Prokopios, on the road, marks the turning. This area of Naxos, called the **Tragea**, is one vast basket of fruit and flowers. Olives, citrus trees, figs, grapes and lilac trees spill out of village gardens.

Chalki, 1km (½ mile) beyond the Damarianos turning, is the site of the 9th-century Church of the Virgin Protothronos ('First Enthroned'), directly opposite the kiosk on the main road through town. Adjacent is the Grazia Tower, with its heraldic shield, dated 1742, above the portal, once the seat of the Barozzi family. If you want, park near the kiosk and inquire about the location of the priest's house, a short distance up the road from his church. He will open the church for you, if he's available. The 9th- to 13th-century wall paintings, especially the fierce Christ encircled by haloed saints in the dome, and the graceful Annunciation, are exquisite. If the father's away, walk a bit and stretch your legs in Chalki's narrow streets. This is a pristine little village much unchanged since the turn of the century. At the *kafeneion* **O Manolis**, stop in and have a Greek coffee under the shade of a giant lilac tree. (If you do take the five-minute walk to the priest's house, 'Papa Vassilis', and fail to find him in, at least take a moment to smell the roses in his garden and peek at the Papadakis Tower next door, a private residence: the 20th-century Naxians are very comfortable inhabiting their forebears' citadels, at least in warm weather.)

Just outside Chalki, bear right for Filoti and Danakos. The sugar-loaf-like peak on your left is called Fanari, or 'Lighthouse'. The village of **Filoti**, 2½km (1½ miles) above Chalki, is a pyramid of sugarcube houses, yet a very workaday town, nestled below Fanari. The tiny white chapel perched on a peak to your left is sacred to St John (feast day, 9 August) and a two-hour hike from Filoti. Park near the square, shaded by plane trees, and have a bite to eat at the **Pano Yefiri** ('Above The Bridge') Restaurant, run by genial Greek-Canadians. If you're here on 15 August, you can participate in the jubilant celebrations marking the Dormition of the Virgin. (Hikers take note: in Hora at the Zoom Foto Service/International Press shop on the harbour, pick up a copy of Christian Ucke's *Walking Tours On Naxos*. This is the best guide for hardy athletic types with a month or so on the island who want to explore the Tragea further.)

For those with jeeps, there is a poor road to a pristine beach located to the south. It's a 24-km (15-mile) drive for another day, but you'll have the road, the medieval towers en route and, at trek's end, **Kalandos beach**, pretty much to yourselves. Inquire at the Pano Yefira for directions. Of course, it's also possible to reach Kalandos from Agiasos Beach, or from Hora, by boat.

Outside Filoti, on the Apeiranthos road, Mt Zeus, or Zas, a little like Gibraltar in aspect, rises 1,001m (3,284ft) on your left. Beyond Filoti 2½km (1½ miles) is the turning for Danakos. Bear left, staying on the primary road, taking in views of Naxos behind you towards Hora. Over the high saddle of Zas, the Cyclades' highest peak, the sea appears again, and you begin your descent to Apeiranthos, which you enter after another 3km (2 miles). **Apeiranthos**, settled by Cretan immigrants, has a fine Cycladic **museum** (daily 8.30am–1.30pm in summer). Park near the end of town where the Church of the Virgin abuts the main road, opposite a war memorial. From here, simply set out on foot along the main, marble-paved village street. Yiorgios Kastrisios (tel: 61260), the curator of the museum, is a knowledgeable, affable gentleman: call for an appointment if you arrive out of season. The museum is a storefront located some 250m (800ft) from the war memorial, just beyond the Church of St Anthony, with its sheltering plane tree. If you're interested in visiting caves where the makers of these Cycladic artefacts lived, call the wonderful Zorbas Grazias (tel: 61339) in Apeiranthos, and tell him Elizabeth

In Apeiranthos

Cottage industry

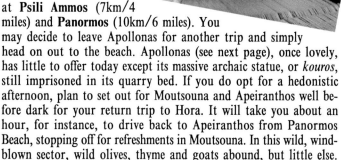

sent you. Zorbas will also be instrumental in finding you accommodation should you wish to return again to Apeiranthos for a longer stay.

East of the village 12km (7 miles) is the seaside village of **Moutsouna**, for those of you who decide on an afternoon at the beach rather than a circuit of the island via Apollonas. In the distance, on your drive down to the sea, you can see the islets of Makares, and beyond, Donoussa. Down the east coast below Moutsouna are fine beaches at **Psili Ammos** (7km/4 miles) and **Panormos** (10km/6 miles). You may decide to leave Apollonas for another trip and simply head on out to the beach. Apollonas (see next page), once lovely, has little to offer today except its massive archaic statue, or *kouros*, still imprisoned in its quarry bed. If you do opt for a hedonistic afternoon, plan to set out for Moutsouna and Apeiranthos well before dark for your return trip to Hora. It will take you about an hour, for instance, to drive back to Apeiranthos from Panormos Beach, stopping off for refreshments in Moutsouna. In this wild, wind-blown sector, wild olives, thyme and goats abound, but little else.

The glittering, charcoal-grey stone here is emery, used by ancient Naxians to polish marble statuary, and was once one of Naxos's primary exports.

If you've had enough of beaches on Mykonos, and opt for the **northern trek** including Apollonas, set out north from Apeiranthos, past giant oaks whose acorns are used for feed in this region. All along your winding route, it's a wise idea to sound your horn before blind curves. About 5km (3 miles) out of Apeiranthos is a small saddle of land occupied by the little Church of Stavros Keramotis. Here, you can look both west and east and see

Apeiranthos alleyway

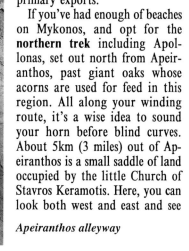

the sea. Follow the signs for Apollonas, ignoring turnings to the right for small villages such as Liona. After about 3½km (2¼ miles), you will enter the village of Koronos, spilling down the hill and best seen from a distance. The village of Skado is next on your route. Outside Skado, take the lower, faster Mesi/Apollonas road, passing through little Mesi, where the asphalt peters out for a while: road works are in progress all over Naxos. Twelve kilometres (7 miles) along your way, you pass a stream and springs along the road where a profusion of pomegranate trees, lemons, banana palms and reeds mark the course of the torrent to the sea. The land to the north is heavily terraced here. The soil-poor islanders create these 'land dams' to stop erosion and catch a little arable earth in their stone nets.

Precisely 1½km (1 mile) on, take the upper left turning for the *kouros*. About 600m (2,000ft) further, there's a small blue sign on your left. Park here and walk up a flight of 65 ugly cement steps. Two minutes up is **Apollonas's** enormous 10½-m (34-ft) long **stone giant**, lying on his back in the marble quarry where, for some unknown reason, he was abandoned by his Cycladic sculptors in the 6th century BC. After clambering around the *kouros*, which probably depicted Dionysos, give Apollonas itself a miss and continue straight on, taking the northern coast road back towards Hora.

Rounding the cape, to the north is Mykonos in the distance. Naxos is desolate and windswept here, the north littoral taking the brunt of the winter storms, but this is the beauty of the barren Cyclades. On this dusty road 8½km (5 miles) along is **Agia**, a stark medieval fortress tower worth a stop to inspect but now abandoned on its perch above the sea.

Eight km (5 miles) beyond Agia is a turning for **Abram**, where on hot, windless days the gravel beach is inviting and there's a small taverna and hotel. On your left, 5km (3 miles) on, is the Monastery of the Virgin Faneromeni, dating from the 17th

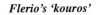

Flerio's 'kouros'

century. It is a photogenic and eccentric structure much frequented by cats.

Some 9km (5½ miles) further south, you will see a fertile plain, dotted with orange groves, pass a small bridge and enter the busy town of **Engares**. There's a huge, modern wind turbine generating power for Hora on a hill above the distant village of Gallini. Drive 10km (6 miles) more, and you will enter Hora, the road intersecting the harbour near the bus terminus.

PAROS

On Naxos, buy ferry tickets for Paroikia, Paros (and anywhere else) from Despina Kitini or Captain Dendrinos (see *Practical Information* for travel agencies). The crossing on the plush *Poseidon Express* takes approximately one hour. If you've made no reservations or wish to rent a car, turn left from the ferry pier and walk to the Avant Travel Agency and Budget Rent A Car. Paros, unlike Naxos, does not bristle with villages, nor is it, like Mykonos, so studiedly touristic, though it attracts more visitors in summer. Paros is mysterious and laid-back, the perfect place to unwind in spring and autumn.

9. Paroikia

Breakfast at the Café Nostos Creperie; the Church of Ekaton-tapyliani; the Old Agora; view from the Church of Constantine and Helen; by caique to the beaches of Krios and/or Kaminia; return to town for dinner at the Tamarisko Garden Restaurant.

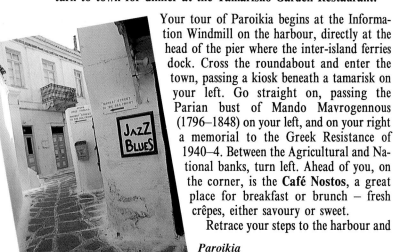

Your tour of Paroikia begins at the Information Windmill on the harbour, directly at the head of the pier where the inter-island ferries dock. Cross the roundabout and enter the town, passing a kiosk beneath a tamarisk on your left. Go straight on, passing the Parian bust of Mando Mavrogennous (1796–1848) on your left, and on your right a memorial to the Greek Resistance of 1940–4. Between the Agricultural and National banks, turn left. Ahead of you, on the corner, is the **Café Nostos**, a great place for breakfast or brunch – fresh crêpes, either savoury or sweet.

Retrace your steps to the harbour and

Paroikia

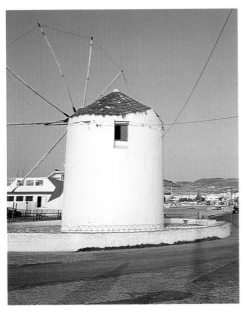

turn right at the mill, then right again before the chapel of St Nicholas, down a tree-lined street abutting the municipal park. At the vertex of this triangular park, next to a little stand of pines and cedar, is the white facade (with tiled roof) of the **Church of the Hundred Doors**, the **Ekatontapyliani**, dedicated to the Virgin. By any name, and it has several locally, this church has been in continual use since it was founded in the 6th century AD. Tradition has it that St Helen, mother of the Emperor Constantine, rode out a storm on Paros and so vowed to found a church on the island, a promise the Emperor Justinian later realized. The cloister and garden post-date the original church by a century, erected to protect the holy fathers from pirates.

The church proper, within its sugary, whitewashed shell, is stark, its naked stones a beautiful, mottled and buttery grey. In contrast, massive gilt chandeliers, huge silver-chased ikons of Christ and the Virgin (draped in *tamata*, gold and silver votive offerings dedicated to the Holy Family in return for answered prayers) and the lacey tracery of the marble altar screen create a rich interior counterpoint to the austerity of the architecture. To the north of the structure, the small chapel of St Nicholas, oldest of the church's several shrines dedicated to various saints, incorporates ancient columns of Parian marble. In the baptistery, to the west of the main church, is a sunken font used for immersion baptism and shaped in the form of a huge cross. Should your visit to Paros coincide with the commemoration of the Dormition of the Virgin, on 15 August, you will witness the island's, and Ekatontapyliani's, greatest feast day.

Inside Ekatontapyliani

Outside the church, turn left, then right (unless you wish to make time for Paros' **archaeological museum**, some 50m/160ft up the hill to your left; daily, 8.30am–2.30pm; Monday and holidays, closed; Sunday, free admission). About 20m (65ft) from the corner, pass between the

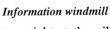

churches of St Nicholas, on your left, and Christ the Saviour, on your right. Go straight on past a reed and timber archway on your right: further on, mount a stair and go straight on across an eccentric little square, passing a fountain dated 1777 and the Church of the September Virgin on your right; then the Church of the Three Saints on your left. At the next left turning, look left. This is the little street leading to the Tamarisko Garden Restaurant, clearly signposted, where you will be returning for dinner. Pass by the arched entrance to Agorakritou Street. You will intersect the main shopping street of the **Old Agora** here. Turn right, then immediately left. Three shops here – Svouna, Ammos Jewellery and, next door, with its huge amphora, the Paros Art Gallery – are the best places to shop in the Old Agora, especially the latter, which features arts and crafts.

Retrace your steps back out to the Poldo Snack Bar (two doors up to the left is the good Ragousis Bakery), and turn right down into the town. This is the main shopping thoroughfare, **Lohagos Kortianos Street**. Look left at an arched building, the **House of Evanthia Damias**, with its two odd relief sculptures worked into the walls – undated

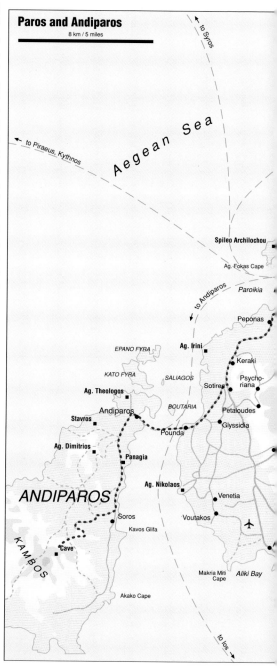

Paros and Andiparos

8 km / 5 miles

to Syros

Aegean Sea

to Piraeus, Kythnos

to Andiparos

Spileo Archilochou

Ag. Fokas Cape

Paroikia

Peponas

EPANO FYRA

Ag. Irini

Keraki

KATO FYRA

SALIAGOS

Psycho-riana

Sotires

Ag. Theologos

BOUTARIA

Petaloudes

Andiparos

Glyssidia

Stavros

Pounda

Ag. Dimitrios

Panagia

Ag. Nikolaos

ANDIPAROS

Venetia

Soros

Voutakos

Kavos Glifa

Cave

K A M B O S

Makria Miti Cape

Aliki Bay

Akako Cape

to Ios

— though the fountain on your right, several metres further on, is another of the elegant local waterworks.

Turn right up the stairs here to reach Paroikia's **Kastro** quarter, dead ahead of you, the drums of the ancient Parian temples to Apollo and Demeter worked into its medieval walls. Today, the Frankish fortress forms a massive impromptu dovecote, so beware

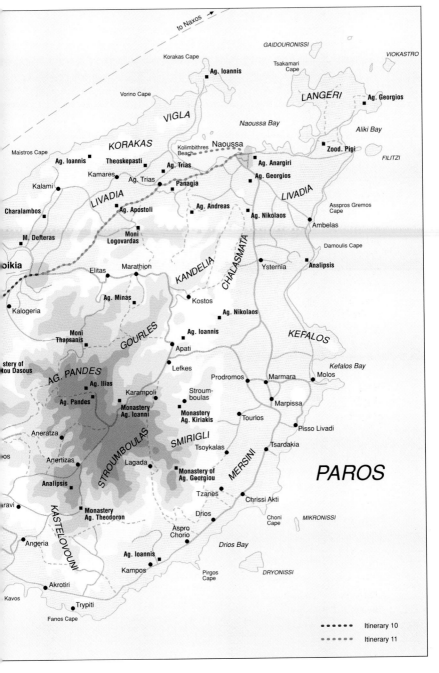

aerial offerings. Turn right and circumnavigate what's left of the Venetian citadel, turning right towards the port now for the Church of Saints Constantine and Helen, then up a flight of steps to your left. The broad terrace before the church, on either side of the 300-year-old structure, contains the marble foundations of the 7th-century BC **Temple of Apollo**, its upper structures long since cannibalised for later public works.

Retrace your path downhill to the main shopping street and amble at your leisure through the Old Agora, chockablock with boutiques and tourist tat, but garlanded with Rose of Sharon and oleander. When you tire of the press of flesh, return to the port and take a caique across the bay for a swim at Paroikia's decent town beaches, **Krios** or **Kaminia**. In the evening, after 7pm, repair to the **Tamarisko Garden Restaurant** or the **Levanti Restaurant** for dinner. (Good places to watch the sunset or for after-dinner drinks, are the Pebbles Piano Bar or the Ouzerie, both on the harbourfront near the Town Hall.) Don't neglect the good Parian wines this evening: the red Paros label, Crevelier rosé, or white Nisiotissa.

10. Morning on the Tiny Isle of Andiparos

Ferry from Paroikia or, alternatively, by bus or hire car from Paroikia to Pounta, then ferry to Andiparos island; bus trip to underground cave; swimming or snorkelling.

You can catch a caique from Paroikia for the small island just west of Paros, Andiparos, from May to the first week in October. The voyage takes about 45 minutes, and takes you past tiny Saliagos islet, once, with Andiparos and Paros, a single land mass. It was here that the first human settlements of the Cycladic era were unearthed. An alternate route to Andiparos is to rent a car and take the westernmost road out of Paroikia, but I advise taking the bus (departures in summer, 7am–10pm) which heads out of town following signs for Naoussa, and turns right near the Ekatontapyliani.

Signs for **Pounta** are abundant. The 8-km (5-mile) drive takes you through Paroikia's uninteresting outskirts, by package-infested hotels on tiny west-coast coves. On a rise just beyond Paroikia, you will see Andiparos on your right as well as the tiny islet where the Chapel of St Spyridon perches. Bear right downhill for Pounta. Among the other barren islets mid-channel is Saliagos, second on your right behind private Revmatonisi, which belongs to the Goulandris shipping family. The car ferry schedule coordinates with that of the Paroikia buses, so don't tarry when leaving the bus.

The crossing from Pounta takes about five minutes, and the ferry

Boats afloat

A place in the sun

carries cars as well as passengers. On calm days, you can look down into the channel water and see ancient walls, proof of the earlier unity of these islands.

Despite the Scandinavians' discovery of Andiparos, there are still no cars allowed within the main town, and sufficient beaches and coves around the island to afford privacy if you're seeking it. If you bring a car, take the eastern road south out of **Andiparos Town**. The beach hamlet of **Soros** has a small taverna; **Aghios Georgios** is a village with several tavernas. Be prepared for the asphalt to peter out once you leave Andiparos proper.

Of course, in addition to the beaches, the main attraction on Andiparos is its **ancient cave**, 9km (6 miles) from Andiparos Town and open April till mid-October. A special bus awaits visitors alighting from the ferries and departs on schedule; the fare includes entrance to the cave. The mouth of the cave is 50m (160ft) up a rocky hill, where there are gorgeous views to the south of Ios (left), Sikinos (ahead) and Folegandros (right).

Discovered, say locals, by the Parian poet Archilochos, and visited in Hellenistic times by several of Alexander the Great's generals, the cave is 125m (410ft) deep, plumbed by 409 precipitous steps with iron guard rails, constructed in 1936 (and seemingly not improved since). At the foot of these treacherous steps is the signature of King Otto, dated 1840. In 1673, there was an amazing Catholic mass celebrated in the great chamber here by a French bishop/consul. Two hundred celebrants made the descent, causing much breakage of the slow-growing stalactites and stalagmites. German bombs also wrought havoc here in World War II. If you arrive out of season, call the cave's guard in Andiparos Town, tel: 0284 61315, and ask Mr Vassilis Patellis to arrange your visit.

Mr Frangiskos Morakis at Morakis Tours (tel: 0284 61346, 61390; fax: 0284 61349) in Andiparos Town, will be helpful in arranging transport and accommodation. If you decide to have lunch in Paroikia, head up the main market street and turn left at the eucalyptus tree. **Makis's Restaurant** has healthy home cooking.

Either by public bus, or hire car (if you plan to consume Parian wine, take the bus) to Naoussa; an afternoon on a beautiful, busy beach; dinner; plus a sample of 'souma' at the Kargas ouzerie.

Naoussa has succumbed, like Lindos on Rhodes, to rampant over-development, all the more reason to visit it early or late in the season. By bus from Paroikia, the uninteresting drive across the north-eastern part of the island to the northern port village takes 20 minutes. Over the course of the uninspiring 10-km (6-mile) journey, you will pass, on your right, the precipitously placed **Monastery of the 'Penniless Saints'**, the Aghoii Anargyri, Cosmas and Damian. Nearer Naoussa, again on your right, is the huge **Longovarda Monastery**, dedicated to the Virgin of the Life-giving Spring, but closed to women. From the bus terminus in Naoussa, turn right towards the sea under the arches (called the Yefira, or bridge) through which runs a channelled stream, and find the main port.

Around to your right is the seaside **Chapel of St Nicholas** and, across from it, facing onto the working fishermen's port-within-the-port, Barbaroussa, an ouzerie serving the locals' version of homemade whisky, called *souma*. The octopus drying in the sun and the fresh mackerel go well with the Parian spirit.

Round the fishermen's harbour and return to the main port. From here, board a caique for the nearby beaches of **Kolimbithres**, with its dramatic rock formations, **Monastiri** (named for the Monastery of St John atop the bluff), **Langari** or **Santa Maria**. In summer, there are departures from 10am till 6 or 7pm.

Returning to Naoussa, if you're hungry, there are several good restaurants to choose from. On the corner opposite the post office is **O Christos**, a pricey garden restaurant behind a blue-black door on Mando Mavrogennous Street. Or, past the police station, is **Pervolaria**, with its navy and red gate, another place for well-heeled gourmets. Below the Pantanassa, about half-way back to the bus terminus, **Le Carre Restaurant Bar** is a little livelier and less formal. And, if you gave the *souma* a miss in the heat of the sun, do try some before heading back to Paroikia.

Activity in Naoussa's harbour

Santorini

The romantic approach to Santorini, called Thera by the Greeks, is by sea. Take either an afternoon or night ferry, preferably the *Poseidon Express* from Paros, and splurge on a first-class cabin. Be sure to be on deck about 45 minutes before arriving, to enjoy the view of the cliffs. You will actually steam into the giant caldera, or volcanic bay, formed when the island erupted in c.1628BC. If you arrive in the wee hours, you'll usually be allowed to stay on board till morning. In summer, buses meet the ferries at all hours; it is crucial to have booked accommodation. Your hotelier can arrange transport or advise about connections.

I recommend two travel agencies. For both your accommodation and touring needs, contact Eftyhis 'Felix' Markozannes at Markozannes Tours/Travel Agency in Phira, tel: 0286 22813/22987; fax: 0286 23107, or Karvounis Tours in Oia, tel: 0286 71209/71205.

12. Around the Island

Walk from Imerovigli or Firostefani to Phira; museums and breakfast, or lunch, in town; bathe at Kamari, Vlihada or Perivolos beaches; sunset drinks at Franco's Bar in Phira; dinner at the Sphinx; bars in Phira. Remember your bathing gear.

Just once, perhaps, during your stay, you might want to get up early – dawn is breathtaking on Santorini – and take the cliffside walk to Phira, the island's capital town, from your villa/hotel at Imerovigli or Firoste-fani. (From Oia, it's just too long and warm a trek.) If you've taken my advice and are staying in one of the villa complexes on the caldera, you've experienced traditional Santorinian architecture first-hand – the *skafta*, or

Sailing into Santorini

Painted pathway

barrel-vaulted dwellings carved into the cliff. All along your walk this morning, you will see honeycombs of these dwellings, designed by the islanders to afford protection from earthquakes on this seismically active island.

As you make your way along the mostly concrete-paved track, you will constantly have the caldera on your right. From Imerovigli, you will see, to the far right, the inhabited islet of Therasia. Next is the fat black star of the volcanic crater itself, an islet called Nea Kamenia (New Burnt Island), with Palea Kamenia (Old Burnt Island) and tiny Aspro (White) behind it. As the crescent-shaped island of Santorini itself curves around to the southwest, you can see the village of (modern) Akrotiri near the end of the crescent. On a five-minute walk south of Imerovigli, on a clear day, you will see, left to right, the islands of Ios, Amorgos, Anidro and Anaphi in the distance.

Circumnavigate the huge, blue-domed **Convent of St Nicholas** on your right (daily 8am–noon and 2.30–5pm, closed Wednesday and Friday; modest attire) and take the path through thistle-covered dry stone walls. Five minutes further and you enter **Firostefani**. The elegant grey and white dome on your right belongs to the Roman Catholic Church of St Mark. The Greek Orthodox Church

of St Gerasimos, flanked by cedars, is on your left after about 50m (160ft), a wonderful place to celebrate Greek Orthodox Easter. On the little 'square', with its three eucalyptus trees, **To Aktaion** (a 'wine-cook-shop') serves great Greek coffee. From here, you have a matchless view, seawards, of Therasia, and the striated knob of Skaros, once the site of the island's medieval capital, to your right behind Imerovigli.

As you walk, the northern tip of Santorini, and the village of Oia, become visible behind Skaros. The ochre facade of the RC Church of the Virgin makes a nice place to take a breather on one of the blue benches. Ten minutes below Firostefani, you

Cat on a hot white roof

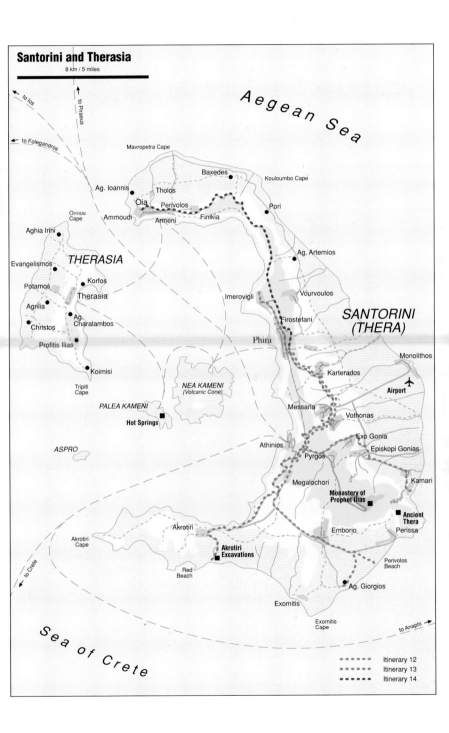

Santorini and Therasia

8 km / 5 miles

Aegean Sea

to Ios
to Piraeus
to Folegandros

Mavropetra Cape
Baxedes
Kouloumbo Cape
Ag. Ioannis
Tholos
Oia
Perivolos
Pori
Ammoudi
Armeni
Finikia

Ormos Cape
Aghia Irini
THERASIA
Ag. Artemios

Evangelismos
Korfos
Potamos
Imerovigli
Vourvoulos
Therasia
Agrilia
Firostefani
Christos
Ag. Charalambos
Phira
SANTORINI (THERA)
Profitis Ilias
Koimisi
Monolithos
Tripiti Cape
Karterados
NEA KAMENI
(Volcanic Cone)
Airport
PALEA KAMENI
Messaria
Hot Springs
Vothonas
ASPRO
Exo Gonia
Athinios
Episkopi Gonias
Pyrgos
Kamari
Megalochori
Monastery of Prophet Ilias
Akrotiri
Ancient Thera
Akrotiri Cape
Emborio
Perissa
Akrotiri Excavations
Red Beach
Perivolos Beach
Exomitis
Ag. Giorgios
Exomitis Cape
to Crete
to Anaphi

Sea of Crete

········· Itinerary 12
········· Itinerary 13
●●●●●●● Itinerary 14

61

round a bend and see Phira to the south, behind it the pozzoulana quarry (volcanic, pumice-like stone was mined here), and Mt Profitis Ilias in the distance. Be sure to bear right, always along the cliff face. The huge, rose-coloured building on your left is the Nomikos Foundation Congress Hall where, in early September, the Santorini Music Festival's performances of classical music are staged.

Pass the Flame of the Volcano restaurant on your left, and the ochre, grey and puce Church of St Stylianos seaward. Look down to your right to see the cable cars, and the tiny port (for yachts and caiques) of Mesa Yialos. Here, the path turns inland. Pass the cable car entrance and proceed to the **Archaeological Museum of Thera** (daily 8.30am–3pm; closed Monday). The museum contains much to see. There is a fine collection of late 6th-century BC Attic Black Figure vases here. A late 7th-century BC amphora with a relief of a Cycladic workshop and a graceful, long-necked bird is also worth seeking out. The archaic *kouroi*, made of Parian marble, are faceless but elegant.

Outside the museum again, bear right, uphill, following signs for the **Catholic Cathedral**. Turn left for the cathedral, dedicated to St John the Baptist. To the right is the Dominican Convent of St Catherine, where the sisters pray 24 hours a day.

Retrace your steps and turn left downhill, entering the side door

Phira transport

to the **Megaron Gyzi Museum** (daily May to end-September, 10.30am–1.30 pm and 5–8pm; till end-October 10am–4pm; closed public holidays), a 17th-century mansion spared in the 1956 earthquake. The museum is a holding of the Catholic bishopric and exhibits a fine collection of engravings, documents, paintings and prints featuring Santorinian landscapes, pre-quake photographs and island maps from the 16th to 19th century. Don't miss the Icon Workshop here, which displays the work of Katerina Ioannidou (tel: 0286 23077/82676). Exit the museum from its front gates and turn right down E E Stavros Street into the town of **Phira**. About 100m (330ft) on, there's a little turning left and you'll find Cava Renos on the corner, a good place to buy Santorinian wines. Restaurant Nikolaos, for future reference, is just down Stavros Street on your left. Almost immediately, you pass the Kira Thira Jazzbar on your right, and a few doors down, Nikos Silaides's **Every Day** café, where you can stop for a much-deserved

Child's play

breakfast of Lavazza coffee and a brioche or croissant or all three. If you've had a late start and it's lunchtime, cut back to Restaurant Nikolaos for fresh fish, if available, or Greek favourites such as moussaka or stuffed tomatoes.

If it's still early, you may want to take some time to shop in Phira. Turn right out of Every Day down Stavros Street. At the corner, you may want to pick up some fruit for later on. Turn right then, and head uphill towards the cliff all the way to the northern end of Ypapantis Street for foreign newspapers, or turn left for Phira's best shopping. As you walk south on Ypapantis, you will pass Greco Gold on your right, the Gallery Zoi on your left on the corner and the Palia Fabrika Art Gallery, followed by Mati (see *Shopping*).

At the far southern end of Phira is the **Greek Orthodox Cathedral** and, across from it, and downhill, for future reference, the restaurants of Alexandria and the Sphinx. If the cathedral is open, take a look inside and ask to be shown the frescoes by Christophoros Assimis, the painter whose work is featured at Palia Fabrika. (For enthusiasts, Assimis also painted the interior frescoes in the church in Exo Gonia village.) Turn downhill at Mati into Phira's mini-shopping mall, the Fabrica Shopping Centre (a good range of foreign newspapers are also available here, as well as the telephone exchange or OTE).

You now have a choice of bathing options. You can take a public bus from Phira (a nightmare excursion in July and August, however, when the buses are packed with teenagers) to **Kamari beach**, a 10-km (6-mile) ride through the countryside to the black east-coast strand. Alternatively, you can head to Drive In Rent A Car (tel: 0286 25225/ 25377; fax: 0286 25377) and rent a very small car from George Laskaris (you will need a super-compact to pass through the narrow streets of Megalochori). This done, you can head for the less populous beaches of **Perivolos**, **Aghios Giorgios** and **Vlihada** on the south coast. During September and October, these beaches are all but empty.

Kamari beach

On the terrace

Ask the friendly people at Drive In to point you south and proceed out of Phira towards Karterados and Messaria, passing Phira's clinic after 100m (330ft) and, shortly after, a petrol station. Stay on the main road, lined with whitewashed eucalyptus trees. After almost 3km (2 miles), you will reach a crossroads. Turn left for Kamari, if you wish, but the best beaches are straight on. (Those who are already staying here at Messaria will have seen the **Archontikó Argyroú** house museum; others can take a short detour and ask locals for **To Archontikó Argyroú**. This neo-classical mansion, a freeze-frame of a wealthy, 1860 wine-grower's cultured lifestyle, is a must.)

About 1km (¾ mile) on, there are some *skafta* chapels to your right, their entrances heavily whitewashed. This is Santorini's grape-growing region. There are miles and miles of grapes to the south now, the rich volcanic soil creating a delicious harvest for the Boutari winery and the wine collective. To your right there are dramatic views of Phira, Oia and the caldera; 3½km (2¼ miles) further, and you reach the turning for Pyrgos. If you're visiting at Easter, check with your travel agent regarding the weird festivities during which an effigy of Judas Iscariot is hanged, then shot.

Pass on by Pyrgos, following signs for Perissa. After about 1½km (1 mile) turn left through a pistachio grove into **Megalochori** for a scenic detour through this picturesque village. There's no need to stop unless the spirit moves you or unless you want a bite to eat at **Taverna Gero Manolis**, opposite the Church of the Virgin (tel: 0286 81027), but proceed straight on and back out onto the main road. (Don't try this detour on 1 July, the Virgin's Feast Day, when the village is crowded.) Turn left into the main road and proceed 700m (½ mile). Make note, for later, of the turning for Akrotiri and Red Beach (about 9km/6 miles out of Phira). On your right, you'll see the Akron Art Studio/Gallery, where you can see Aspasia and Dimitris produce copies of the Santorini wall paintings.

Less than 1km (½ mile) further is the turning for **Vlihada**, 3km (2 miles) west and a black volcanic family beach in season. You can investigate Vlihada, then return to the main road and proceed southeast for the Aghios Giorgios and Perivolos turnings. (At the Vlihada/Perissa road junction, the village of Pyrgos is dead ahead, Megalochori to the left, and Emborio, over the rise, to your right. The Monastery of the Prophet Elijah, at 566m/1,857ft, to your right, is closed to the public.)

After about 1½km (1 mile), bear right for Perivolos and Aghios Giorgios. After a short distance the asphalt peters out for those bound for **Aghios Giorgios**. I advise bearing left for **Perivolos**. The turning's a bit further down the road. In late spring and autumn, this tamarisk-lined beach, with its deep, clean water and humble tavernas, is wonderful. The 369-m (1,210-ft) high promontory on your left is the site of Ancient Thera, to which there are guided coach tours (arranged through major travel agencies in Phira). It's a dramatically

Octopus 'n' ouzo

situated Hellenistic town, accessible from Kamari, but a guide is essential for an all-around understanding.

After an afternoon on the beaches, head back to Phira to watch the sunset from Franco's Bar. For dinner, repair to the **Sphinx** (see *Eating Out*) and, afterwards, to the lively **Blue Note Pub** or the sophisticated **Kira Thira Jazzbar**, according to your tastes.

13. Akrotiri and Red Beach

A morning excursion to a 2nd millennium BC town; a fish lunch and then a red-pebbled cove.

For this and the following itinerary you will need to rent a car. I recommend Drive In Rent A Car in Phira, adjacent to the new police station (tel: 0286 25225; fax: 0286 25377). Fax ahead so the car will be waiting for you at the airport or port, or ask your hotelier to arrange for your car to be delivered to the hotel.

By car, follow the directions for the previous itinerary and proceed to the Akrotiri/Red Beach turning, about 9km (5 miles) south of Phira. Turn right here and head towards the southwestern tip of the island. A little further on, there's a ruined mill on the right-hand side, a great place to photograph the caldera (give the Panorama Restaurant a miss). This may be the single best view in the Cyclades.

Follow signings for the archaeological site and proceed straight through

Akrotiri's 'Boxing Boys'

drab **modern Akrotiri**. Proceed slowly: this is a dangerous stretch of road. About 4km (3 miles) from the main road turning, you reach the site of **Ancient Akrotiri** (daily 8.30am–3pm, closed Monday; entrance fee, students free). If you have done your reading, the site makes more sense. (*Santorini: A Guide to the Island and its Archaeological Treasures* by Dr Christos Doumas is good background.) Additionally, an acquaintance with the Akrotiri wall paintings in the Archaeological Museum in Athens provides a more graphic picture of the attainments of the residents of this 2nd millennium BC town. Some artefacts from Akrotiri can also be seen in the archaeological museum in Phira, opposite the cable car station.

As you enter the site, you will see the **Techines Road**, the largest section of the road thus far excavated by the Greek *ephor* of this dig, Dr Christos Doumas. The dwellings here were two-storeyed and it was here that the 'frescoes' of the antelopes and the Boxing Boys were unearthed. Giant *pithoi* (storage jars for oil, wine and staple grains) line the walls of these structures. **Building Delta** is further on, a two- or three-storeyed complex containing a mill and pottery workshop. Here were the wall paintings of the lilies.

Ancient Akrotiri

A flyover bridge affords you a panoramic view of Akrotiri, though the extent of the town is still not fully known. Over the bridge is the *pithoi* storeroom, where huge ceramic containers for barley, barley flour and seeds stood. Palaeobotanists have been able to reconstruct the Akrotirians' diet and agricultural production from ancient samples found *in situ*. Here, too, was the three-storeyed **House of the Ladies**, appropriately named on account of the murals of ample-bosomed, raven-haired Santorinians of 3,500 years ago. The **Triangle Square**, with its elaborate residences, once ornamented with paintings of an enormous fleet, fishermen and bathers, is the most impressive area excavated thus far. The lavatory and sophisticated drainage system reflect an advanced, bourgeois culture of merchant seamen (and artists!). Near the Mill House Square is the grave of Dr Spyridon Marinatos, the Greek archaeologist who was first to dig here following tips by Messrs Pelekis and Alvanitis, both local men who suspected great things underfoot.

Exiting the site, turn left to the beach. There are two good tavernas here on the sea serving fresh fish, if it's lunchtime. (I recommend the Fish Tavern Dolphins, tel: 0286 81151.) Otherwise, you can either board a caique for the 10-minute trip to **Red Beach** or drive over the ridge and park, then walk down to this exotically red-pebbled cove.

Red Beach is pretty, empty in spring or autumn, and absolutely everyone takes home some of the brick-red volcanic pebbles.

Early evening drive to Oia; sunset at the Fanari Villas Bar; dinner at 1800, or return to Phira.

From the Phira town limits, it's a 10-km (6-mile) drive to **Oia**, which takes approximately 25 minutes. Enquire of your hotelier what time sunset is and allow plenty of time to reach Oia.

This is one of the most beautiful, tortuous drives in the Aegean; make sure you sound your horn before blind curves, and do not try to negotiate this drive on a full tank of Santorinian wine. From Phira, on past Imerovigli, you have a view of the caldera at various points. Passing the waist of the island, you will see the sea on both sides, the high 250–300m (820–980ft) topography becomes stunningly volcanic, and the long flat plain of eastern Santorini – probably what the entire island looked like prior to 1500BC – stretches off to your right.

After you enter the signed town limits, continue on about another 1½km (1 mile) and bear left up into the parking/bus terminus square. After parking out of the way of the public bus, head up into the village following signs for the youth hostel and Karvounis Tours. Turn left up beside Oia's beautiful blue-domed Church of the Virgin. Oia's blue domes must be among the best-loved and most familiar sights in the Aegean Islands, and justly so. Note the typical Oian architecture: pastel and red-pebble-studded walls reinforced with iron beams. (Oia was completely levelled in the disastrous 1956 earthquake.)

When you reach the main, marble-paved caldera road, Nicholas Nomikos Street, turn right by Karvounis Tours and pass the **Church of the Cross** on your left, which is one of the most photographed buildings in Greece. The Art Gallery opposite carries some very fine realistic

Oia

Sunset on Oia

landscapes. Ten metres (33ft) further on your right is the **1800 Restaurant**, a good place to eat later on.

When you reach a Y-junction, head up to the right towards the Kyklos Restaurant. You will see, out to your left, the **Goulas quarter**, ravaged in the quake and an eerie reminder of Oians lost in that catastrophe. Head off to your right, still following signs for Kyklos, and ask the locals the way to the **Fanari Villas**, located below the mill. The terrace of these idyllic *skafta*, with their intimate bar, is the perfect place to watch the sunset behind Therasia. You may dine at 1800, or make your way back along the road to restaurants in Phira.

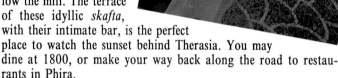

15. Volcanic Voyage

By ferry to the volcano's still-smoking cone in the middle of the caldera. Wear sturdy walking shoes and a hat, and carry along a bottle of water.

There are numerous organised tours, by small ferry or caique, of the caldera, Therasia island and the volcanic crater, as well as bathing excursions to Ammoudi and Armeni, the small port/coves beneath Oia. Some of these tours are a gruelling six hours long, not pleasant in the heat of summer. Frankly, there's little of interest on **Therasia**, with its poor pebbly beach and mediocre tavernas. The town is interesting to those who want a glimpse of what Santorini was like in the 1960s, but few foreign visitors decide to stay.

I suggest taking the shortest boat trip available, a 2-hour, afternoon excursion to the crater itself, to see whether a longer voyage touching base all around the vast caldera is of interest to you. The crater offers all the drama this writer could ask for: it's an exciting, shoe-sizzling experience.

Cable cars

Purchase tickets through **Markozannes** travel agency in Phira, and proceed, about half an hour before departure time, to the **Phira Cable Cars**. Donated by Santorinian shipowner Evangelos Nomikos in 1982, the snazzy Austrian-built system carries 36 passengers at a time and, in a recent year, transported some 400,000 people up and down the cliff face – that's 1,000 passengers an hour in high season. The teleferique has largely supplanted Phira's muleteers, who are subsidised by the profitable cable cars. Still, some people prefer the 680-step hike, and others opt for the dependable mules. By speedy cable car, the ascent takes just under 5 minutes: it's 45 lung-bursting minutes on foot.

A Santorini stroll

At 3pm, your ferry (and it may resemble *The African Queen*) departs from the Old Port. Straight up the cliff behind you are Firostefani and Phira, peeking out over the layers of stratified lava. Since this is the only yacht anchorage on the island, you will be manoeuvring among docked yachts and island ferries, as well as immense cruise ships at anchor in the summertime. As you pull away from the port, you will have a 360° view of the caldera which formed when the island blew up. The eruption here dwarfed that of Krakatoa in terms of destruction, decibels and dimensions.

Fifteen minutes later, you reach the islet which is the site of the collapsed **crater**, looking for the world like the set of a Japanese horror movie, c1957. The volcanic rock is piled up in glossy profusion, reddish brown and obviously very, very new. Your craft will drop you off in a tiny port – no amenities – and leave! Make your way uphill to the west along a much-travelled path, scrabbling up steep hills for part of the way, to the sunken cone. The walk up takes about 45 minutes, remember, and is very demanding.

When you reach the rim of the volcano, resist putting your hand down any of the smoking holes. Silly as this warning sounds, some people feel compelled to try this stunt. That's hydrogen sulphide spewing out and the effect on skin is rather like that of putting your paw down the spout of a boiling kettle. You get the feeling here that Santorini's dragon may have been beheaded in c.1628BC, but it's still kicking.

Since the boat tends to leave on schedule, don't dawdle, no matter how fascinating you find the crater. It takes around 15–20 minutes to return to the port.

Shopping

Visitors to the Cyclades may browse in Naxos's and Paros's old agoras to their hearts' content, but serious shoppers will want to confine their efforts and their wallets to Hora, Mykonos and Phira, Santorini.

Mykonos's main town, Hora, has the best shopping in the Aegean. Visitors in search of gorgeous 24-carat creations can do no better than **Lalaounis**, Greece's 'Ambassador of Gold'. This jeweller from

The White Shop, Mykonos

Delphi has shops throughout the country, but the shop in Hora features a wide selection of his current work: there's no need to wait till Athens. **Theodore Roussounellos**, located on Matoyianni Street, is a local jeweller with Cartier and Rolex concessions who specialises in gem-stone-and-gold creations. The two Michaelides family jewellery stores owned by Rhodian Ioannis Michaelides and sons, specialise in gold and seed pearl copies of traditional Greek designs from the last two centuries. Clothing boutiques abound, but Anna Gelou's **White Shop**, which sells nothing but snowy pullovers and domestic articles such as tablecloths and runners in white, is special. **Masakis T-Shirts**, on Yiorgoulis Street, is the place for stylish Ts. Outre Athenian designer **Parthenis** maintains a branch in Alefkandras Square. In search of an original oil, collage or watercolour? Visit Luis Orozco's and Dorlies Schapitz's Orama Gallery (see *Itinerary 5* for details).

Santorini (Thera) is less developed as a shopping mecca, but Phira is fast catching up with Mykonos. Most of the best emporia are located on the caldera side of the capital on Ypapantis Street, **Palia Fabrika** being the best of the lot. Here painter Christophoros Assimis and his wife Eleni pool their talents, offering striking landscape paintings, jewellery and ceramics. The **Zoi Gallery**, also on Ypapantis, features opulent jewellery. In the **Fabrica Shopping Centre**, adjacent to the cathedral in Phira, posh small boutiques abound,

Roussounellos's store

notably **Mati**, with sculptor Iorgos Kypris's small nudes and whimsical bronze fish sculptures. **Pinello** is the T-shirt stop of choice: Harriet Koutsoyanopoulos's designs are hand-painted. **Greco Gold**, also on the caldera, features designs by Athenian jeweller Minas, who once worked with Elsa Peretti (or vice versa) and Byzantine copies in 22-carat gold by Stephanos Keramides. And don't miss Angelo Tsiagkouris's **The Bead Shop**, across from the new museum building in Phira. From hundreds of beads and ornaments, make your own necklaces and bracelets.

In Hora, Naxos, **Popi's Grill** (on the waterfront, an entire lamb turning on a spit in the window), sells Naxian products such as cheese, citron liqueur (made from the leaves of a local citrus fruit); tiny eggplants, cherries and citron conserves, candied in syrup; and Naxian honey. **Takis Probonas's** shop markets fancier versions of these same liqueurs and sweets. On Apollonas Street, in the Old Agora, is **The Loom**, Hora's premier antique and quality souvenir shop, featuring shadow puppets, antique silver belt buckles, Greek sheep's bells and hand-loomed clothing. For copies of the marble idols in the museum, head south in Hora to Protodikeiou Square and **Nicolas**, where they also carry onyx and marble chess tables and ikons. The funky general shopping road in Hora is **Papavassiliou Street**, which runs into the main road to the northern villages. Here are Hora's shoeshops, modest jewellery stores and small tourist shops selling wacky Naxian tat. On Naxos, and throughout the Cyclades, look for Pierre Couteau's striking black-and-white and colour postcards. Couteau, a French photographer, and son of painter Genevieve Couteau, lives on Mykonos. Many of his photographs were used in *Insight Guide: Athens* and *Insight Guide: Greek Islands*.

A good place to begin on Paros is **Heiropiimata** (Hand Poems), also known as the Paros Art Gallery. On Nikos Katris Street in Paroikia's Old Agora quarter, this shop carries Naxian craftspeople's work; most striking are the pottery and ceramics of Monica and Stelios Ghikas, who maintain a workshop you can visit. **Svoura** (The Spinning Top), two doors down, has quality crafts and toys.

The **Teapot**, down an alley across from the Levanti Restaurant in Paroikia, sells Mediterranean spices and herbs, tea and henna. Ask Janet to tell you about all the great-smelling greenery in the shop she and Stelios run.

Oian shops in the evening

Eating Out

Cycladic island cuisine is a variation on the mainland Greek theme, a poor relation of the more opulent diet consumed by the keepers of flocks and orchards. On stony, water-poor Mykonos, Paros and Santorini, the lush peaches of northern Greece, the immense olives of Kalamata, and the fat lambs of Ioannina are not to be found. Naxos, with its fertile and mountainous interior, is the odd-island-out, and serves as bread-basket for its barren neighbours. But even Naxian tables cannot vie with those of the mainland: the island diet reflects island life – spartan, frugal and redolent of the sea. And while all Greek food features strongly the 'Mediterranean triad' of cereals, olives (and their oil) and wine, island fare is closest to the heart-friendly diet-for-life so highly recommended by Western cardiologists. Olive oil supplies most of the islanders' daily fat intake; small fish such as whitebait, eaten whole, or consumed in a light Greek bouillabaise, provide protein; fresh greens, spinach, onions, tomatoes and garlic figure in most recipes; whole grain bread and pasta satisfy hunger; and liberal draughts of wine accompany everything but breakfast. In the villages, what is placed before you is neither expensive nor easy to prepare: what it is, on the other hand, is good for you.

Of course, 30 years of tourism have eroded culinary traditions in the Cyclades as well as the islanders' social, religious and economic heritage. Hora, on Mykonos, Phira and Oia on Santorini, and Paroikia on Paros all harbour Chinese, French or Italian restaurants, or all of the above, in the case of Mykonos. Still, the Greek culture is surprisingly tenacious, and what Mama slaved over and served at home is generally what her children expect to find on their own tables and expect to provide for Mama's grandchildren as well. The Greeks know a good thing when they sit down to it, and the Mediterranean Triad has been a good thing since the days of the *Iliad* and the *Odyssey*.

Greek salad and ouzo

Where To Eat What

Dining in Greece is a specialised affair: one orders one's *metrio* (Greek coffee – don't drink the quarter inch of grounds at the bottom of the thimble) at a *kafeneion;* one finds starters (*mezethes*) and *ouzo,* beer or *retsina* at a *mezethopoleion;* one dines on simple local fare, as the Greeks do, at a *taverna,* the Greek equivalent of the bistro, or heads up-market to a pricier *estiatorion,* or Europeanised restaurant; and, finally, one consumes one's *baklava* or profiterole, at a *zacharoplasteion,* or patisserie. This said, in such towns as Hora on Mykonos and Phira and Oia on Santorini, the traditionally food-segregated eateries exist side by side with what the Greeks call *Fastfoodathika,* generally tourist-trade-spawned dives serving ghastly toasted cheese sandwiches and dubious ice-cream: to be avoided at all costs! As you make your way around Cycladic towns on foot, you will pass a neighbourhood bakery about every third block. Stop in and look around.

Food with a view

Mykonos 'kafeneion'

This is where the Greeks buy, and eat, breakfast and snacks, generally standing up. Try *karidopittes* (walnut muffins) or grape-must flavoured biscuits, *moustoukouloura,* or the old standbys, the *tiropitta,* cheese pie, *spanakopitta,* spinach pie and the *milopitta,* Greece's version of good 'ole apple pie.

The price range denoted here is for a meal for one person and when appropriate, includes a moderately priced bottle of wine. Inexpensive = under 4400 drachmas; Moderate = around 4400 drachmas; Expensive = 4400–11000 drachmas.

Mykonos

EFTHIMIOS EFTHIMIOU'S PATISSERIE
Fl. Zouganeli Street, Hora
For over 40 years, Efthimiou has served up Mykonos's famed 'little baskets' (*kalathakia*) and macaroons in his immaculate sweet shop – for 15 years at this location. (Takeaway only.) Expensive.

L'ANGOLO BAR
Lakka district, Hora
Tel: 0289 24207
From 8am till 2am, this Italian café

is the place for espresso, cappuccino and a quick breakfast, as well as packed lunches for Delos or the beach. Moderate.

NIKOLA'S TAVERNA
Aghia Anna Beach (after Plati Yialos)
Tel: 0289 23566
A locals' favourite: an authentic Greek taverna on a pretty, tiny beach. Moderate.

TAVERNA NIKO'S
Just off the harbour, up from
St. Nicholas church
Tel: 0289 24320
For a quarter of a century, Niko's has made fresh fish and lobster their speciality. Try homemade moussaka, salads with capers and *roka*. Great service. Moderate.

SESAME KITCHEN
Three Wells district, Hora
Tel: 0289 24710

Katrin's

Hazel Fouski is English, and the charming bistro she has established in Hora is a vegetarian's haven, though meat dishes appear on the menu as well. This is my favourite small bar and a great place to sample Greek bottled wines. High season 7pm–1am. Moderate.

KATRIN'S
Aghios Yerasimos district, Hora
Tel: 0289 22169
For 20-odd years, 'Bobbys' has featured pricey French cuisine with a Mykonian twist. Order his seafood starters and finish with chocolate mousse. Mr Giziotis also owns Super Paradise Beach's Coco Bar. High season 7pm–4am. Reservations necessary. Expensive.

MATTHEW TAVERNA
Tourlos (on San Stefanos road)
Tel: 0289 22344, 24984
This is a polished taverna, and the service on the cool terrace is personalised and genuine. Try *Bekri Meze*, a kind of Greek *boeuf bourgignon*, or lamb wrapped in vine leaves. High season noon–1am. Inexpensive to moderate.

LA BUSSOLA
Laka district, Hora
Tel: 0289 26348
Chef Giovanni Marale serves up excellent Genovese dishes, but the pizza is also delicious. Whatever you choose as a main course, be sure to try the Panna Cotta afterwards. Moderate.

SEA SATIN MARKET
Alefkhandra quarter,
directly below the windmills
Absolutely unique waveside restaurant, Sea Satin is open from breakfast until tea-time. Creative, home-made cuisine, Easter until mid-September. Inexpensive.

Discerning dining

Naxos

THE MELTEMI RESTAURANT
Extreme southern end of Hora's waterfront, on the sea. Tel: 0285 22654
The Meltemi's been here some 50 years, serving Greek cuisine, including fresh fish. It's authentic, reserved and very Greek. Easter till end October, all day till midnight. Inexpensive to moderate.

ONIRO RESTAURANT/ROOF GARDEN/BAR
In Hora downhill from Pradounas Square, just outside Kastro quarter
It's the roof garden's view that's an *oniro*, or dream. The food is simply reliable Hellenic/international. Order the *kaloyeros*, eggplant with veal, or *baxes*, which is a vegetarian's delight. Open Easter till end October. Moderate to expensive.

TO KASTRO TAVERNA
On Pradounas Square
Tel: 0285 23078
This is a good place for Greek rabbit stew, or *stifado,* and *exohiko*, a layered pastry with lamb, cheese and vegetables. Easter till end October. Moderate to expensive.

By the way, have breakfast on the harbourfront at the RENDEZ-VOUS patisserie/café or, if you're awaiting a ferry, at the POTIKIAN, across from the bus terminus and near the Naxos Tourist Information Centre.

After dark, head for the little square of Nikiforos Mandilaras, also called Villandoni Square, next to Takis Probonas's liquor store. Late of an evening here, you may have the good fortune to hear guitarists accompanying Naxian men of a certain age singing either distinctive Naxian songs or mainland ballads of the early 20th century.

For rowdier entertainment, head north out of town 3km (2 miles) for Platanos/Bouzouki Greek dancing. Harbourfront bars in Hora, such as the second-storey GREEK BAR, midway down the waterfront, and VEGGERA, a Mykonos clone at the southern end of the port, are good watering holes.

Paros

TAMARISKO GARDEN RESTAURANT
Neos Dromos Street, Paroikia
Tel: 0284 22170
Located in the Old Agora marketplace. Order Pork Stew Tamarisko, mushrooms in sauce, and the dreamy chocolate mousse. March till end-October 7pm onwards. Closed Monday. Moderate.

CAFE NOSTROS CREPERIE
Near the National Bank, Paroikia
Tel: 0284 22105
Mrs Panagaki, the owner, is a delight. Try her homemade apple pielets and crêpes. Come for breakfast, snacks, decent coffee and freshly squeezed fruit juices. Open all year, all day. Inexpensive.

OUZERIE/PSAROTAVERNA BOUDARAKI
Harbour road, Paroikia
Tel: 0284 22297
Situated just before the Pandrossos Hotel, this is a typical Greek ouzerie with drinks and Greek starters such as grilled octopus and fresh sea urchins. Open Easter till early October. Inexpensive.

THE LEVANTI
Old Agora, Paroikia
Tel: 0284 23613
Next to the Vietnamese restaurant called May-Tey, order mixed Lebanese

Paros harbourside

starters, *falafel* and *tabouli*, as well as one of several diverse salads. Open year round; garden in summer and autumn. Expensive.

O CHRISTOS
Opposite the Church of the Panagia Pantanassa, Naoussa
Tel: 0284 51442
Very elegant; very nice. Stick to seafood, their speciality, and expect to pay somewhat more than usual. Expensive.

PERIVOLARIA RESTAURANT
Near Naoussa's police station, and opposite Artio Travel. Tel: 0284 51598
Snails, snitzel and shrimp – take your pick. It's all good. A fancy, international restaurant with a short summer season and pricey (for Greece) rates. Expensive.

Santorini

TAVERNA KATINA COLETTA
Ammoudi, Oia
Tel: 0286 71280
In many people's eyes, the fresh fish, prawns, lobster and Santorini specialities make this the island's best taverna. Easter until October; from lunch until the wee hours.

TAVERNA AMBROSIA
Kamari.
Tel: 0286 32600
Fotis and his Australian wife, Nicki, have been written up in *Vogue* for the exquisite things they do with seafood. Moderate.

TAVERNA PYRGOS
Pyrgos Village
Tel: 0286 31346
This is an elegant restaurant with an unusual view. Order a table-full of their excellent *mezethes,* or starters, especially the smoky aubergine salad. Expensive.

The Karvounis family has been serving seafood, meat-stuffed lettuce leaves and superb tiropittas etc, for 35 years. Lunch here is superb – matched by the view. Moderate.

Mama's Café (at the Blue Note Bar)
Tel: 0286 24211
Surely Mama Irini serves the best US-style breakfasts in Greece: pancakes, french toast and Maxwell House coffee. Inexpensive.

O Kritikos ("Psistaria")
At Yothonas on the airport road.
Tel: 0286 32300
Barbara and Michaelis have brought this taste of Crete to Santorini. Grilled pork, lamb and veal plus speciality meats are featured. Try *saganaki* (fried cheese) and Cretan house wines.

"Mama Irini"

Restaurant Nikolaos
On Stavros Street, parallel to the caldera road, near the Kira Thira Jazzbar in Phira. Tel: 0286 23607
Only traditional Greek food and very fresh fish is served here, simply prepared for reasonable prices; red and white barrel wines. Serving Santorinians for 35 years. I always order the *koliós* fish. Open year round for lunch and dinner. Moderate.

Every Day Cafe
A few doors south of the Kira Thira Jazzbar in Phira
Tel: 0286 24010
Gild the lily and order their chocolate-covered *baklava* with your Lavazza coffee. Open all day long, from (contrary to its name) 20 March until the end of October. Inexpensive.

Neptune
Near the blue-domed Church of the Virgin, Oia
Tel: 0286 71294

For after-hours tippling, you can't beat the Kira Thira Jazzbar, a barrel-vaulted jazz and blues haunt in central Phira, next to Every Day Cafe. Dimitris Tsavdarides brews a mean sangria. Alternatively, Franco's Bar, on the caldera in Phira, has been rated one of the world's best by no less than *Newsweek International.* The tall drinks it serves are works of art; so is the wonderful view. The Blue Note Pub, also in Phira, is one of the current hot spots in town for the (good) beer and rock bunch.

The Kira Thira Jazzbar

Calendar of Special Events

The Greek year is delightfully interrupted by ancient (read pagan, slightly costumed in respectability), Orthodox Christian, and ethnic/historical holidays. For example, on 21 May, the firewalkers, or *Anastenaria,* in the Thracian village of Kosti celebrate the feast of Saints Constantine and Helen by walking barefoot over glowing coals.

On the other hand, in Hora, on Mykonos, your hoteliers, Costas and Eleni, may invite you round for drinks, but you won't find any Anastenaria hotfooting it on the Mykonian waterfront. Still, the Cycladic islanders have remained true to their pagan, Byzantine and revolutionary Greek roots, and those influences can be seen in their undiluted splendour in highland villages, at country chapels and, off season, even in the busy summer resorts whose shops have been boarded up for the winter. Then, the tourist industry hustle recedes, and the Greek character emerges.

While you're there be sure to ask someone to explain the complicated, but fascinating concept of Saints' days (*Paneyiria*).

JANUARY / MARCH

Carnival (*Apokries*), the three-week revel preceding sober Lent, is still celebrated throughout Greece by costumed and merry Greeks and visitors alike. Your hotelier or the local Cycladic Tourist Police office may be able to steer you towards local festivities. Clean Monday, the last day of Carnival, which marks the beginning of the seven weeks of Lent, is especially festive in the Cyclades, when brave souls venture into the sea for their first spring dips and islanders sit at seaside tavernas drinking and eating in the thin spring sunshine.

On 25 March, Independence Day Parades are held in the islands' capital towns to commemorate the beginning of the Greek War of Independence, 1821.

APRIL / JUNE

Easter is a moveable feast, but it almost always falls in April. It is a joyous, passionate event lasting several days. Though it is most moving to celebrate Easter in the more primitive villages of the Cyclades, foreign visitors in the islands for a brief sojourn profit more from attending midnight services in the large main churches of Hora on Mykonos, Phira or Firostefani on Santorini, Paroikia on Paros and Hora on Naxos. At the capital towns' 'cathedrals' (*Mitropoleos*), English-speaking locals will often help guests make sense of the proceedings and then invite them home for the traditional wee-hours-repast of tripe soup, roast lamb and potatoes, Easter bread and red eggs. *Kalo Pascha* (Happy Easter) is about the only one of the traditional Easter greetings most foreigners can manage. (*Christos Anesti*, or 'Christ is risen!' is appropriate just after, but not before, the candles are lighted in the midnight service.)

May Day (1 May) doubles as a workers' holiday and Greece's official spring festival. Islanders flock to the countryside and seashore to make special May wreaths and to lunch, promenade, and dine at countryside and seaside tavernas.

JULY / SEPTEMBER

On the feast day of the Dormition of the Virgin (15 August), pilgrims make their way to the Church of St Mary the Evangelistria on the island of Tinos, although any Cycladic church dedicated to the Virgin will also be celebrating this mid-August feast. Following the church services, there are often bouzouki-blasting revels in the village squares and dancing and feasting till dawn as all the Cycladic Marias, namesakes of the Virgin, entertain their family, friends and, often, new foreign acquaintances.

OCTOBER / DECEMBER

'Ohi' Day (28 October) commemorates the Greeks' resistance (saying '*Ohi!*' or 'No!') to Benito Mussolini in 1940. Military and school parades criss-cross the islands' main towns and villages. Recitations, Greek dances, fireworks and feasting are the order of the day.

Easter celebration

Practical Information

GETTING THERE

By Air

In the Cyclades, Mykonos, Santorini, Paros and, most recently, Syros all have airports. Olympic Airways adds extra flights during summer, when its limited fleet of ageing island hoppers allows. At Easter and in high season, from May to September, it is essential to make prior reservations and confirm them. The fierce *meltemi* winds of summer often disrupt flight schedules, and passengers bumped from regularly scheduled flights are not automatically rescheduled.

Inter-island flights, such as the connections between Santorini and Mykonos, are not always fully documented in Olympic's brochures, so be sure to ask if additional flights have been added on: you may be pleasantly surprised.

Olympic Airways offices:
US: tel: 800-223 1226
London: tel: 0171-409 3400

Montreal: tel: 514-878 9691
Toronto: tel: 416-964 7137
Melbourne: tel: 03-962 92 411
Sydney: tel: 02-925 11 040

By Sea

Cruise ships dock in Piraeus, and sumptuous luxury liners along with plush as well as pedestrian ferries crowd the Mediterranean's busiest harbour, the most frequent port of embarkation for the Cyclades. The summer ferry schedule is mindbogglingly complicated, and weekly updates are photocopied and distributed by the National Tourist Organisation's Syntagma Square office at 2 Karageorgi Servias Street. There are multiple daily sailings to the Cyclades undertaken by several ferry lines in summer and a rich and hectic schedule of interconnecting and overlapping ferries awaits you once you reach your initial destination. Hydrofoils (the Flying Dolphins) and catamarans further enrich the summer stew in the Aegean.

For current information, phone the Piraeus Port Authority (451 1311; for Zea Marina and the hydrofoil 452 7107) or visit any of the small travel agents lining Nikis Street off Syntagma Square in downtown Athens. In most cases, you will be advised to show up on the pier about an hour ahead of your ferry's scheduled departure. Tickets may be purchased on the pier or even from the purser on board the

Approaching Santorini by ferry

vessel. Savvy sailors will pack a lunch of fresh fruit, bottled water and other comestibles for the often day-long voyage ahead. Loo paper, reading material and a deck of cards also come in handy. Deck class travellers should take along windbreakers, sun screen and something to stretch out on.

As with flight schedules, ferry connections are quite often altered by the capricious *meltemi* gales, so prepare to be cheerfully stranded in bad weather: Aegean travellers have been suffering and enjoying such disruptions ever since Odysseus.

TRAVEL ESSENTIALS

When to Visit

In the best of all possible worlds, it would always be either April or September in the Aegean. In April, the Cyclades are carpeted with wild flowers, the air is clear, the beaches are uncrowded, if a little cool for swimming, and the islanders' tempers are as yet unfrayed by the influx of summer visitors. Easter, by the Greek Orthodox calendar, is a marvellous time to visit, and no-one should miss celebrating this best of Greek holidays with the Greeks at least once. From September through October, the weather is still hot during the day, though a bit cooler at night, many of the summer establishments are still open, and sea and ferry connections are plentiful. From November through April, when storms disrupt schedules, travellers may find themselves at the mercy of the winds and sea.

Visas & Passports

A valid passport is sufficient documentation for foreign nationals entering Greece from Australia, Canada, the European Community, New Zealand, and the United States, if you're staying for a period that is under four months long. Other nationals will need visas.

Customs

Visitors arriving with stereo equipment and cameras may be required to have such items recorded in their passports. This is to prevent the sale of untaxed luxury items to Greek nationals. Officials may check

Alternative transport

to make certain you leave with whatever you brought. Note as well that it is considered a grave and punishable offence to remove antiquities, no matter how small, from Greece. You will also not be allowed to depart with over 10,000 drachmas in Greek currency.

Climate

Spring, from late March through May, is unpredictable. By May, temperatures usually climb into the late 20°s Celsius (80°s Fahrenheit). June through September the mercury hovers in the early 30°s Celsius (90°s and low-100°s Fahrenheit), the heat relieved only by a strong but sporadic wind.

Nights are apt to be chilly, even in high summer. Winter rains may set in as early as October, though the sea is still warm and bather-friendly.

MYKONOS CLIMATE	MAY	JUNE	JULY	AUG	SEPT	OCT
AVG NOON TEMP.	25	30	33	33	29	23
AVG DAILY SUN HRS.	9	11	12	11	9	7
AVG WATER TEMP.	18	22	24	24	23	21

Clothing & Essentials

Summer visitors should pack lightweight clothing in natural fabrics; running shoes for the cobbled Cycladic streets, and sea-urchin-proof shoes for the sea; sunscreen and a beach towel; sunglasses and a sun hat; one modest outfit in which to visit churches; several bikinis, or parts thereof, for the beach; and regalia appropriate for the hottest nightclubs in Europe. Spring and winter visitors should expect and prepare for blustery, cold, wet days outdoors, and damp, chilly nights indoors. A sleeping bag comes in handy on ferries any time and in winter everywhere. Be sure to pack sufficient supplies of prescription drugs. I always include a compass, a police whistle and, for those moonless evenings, a mini-torch.

Electricity

Power sockets are rated at 220 volts AC, and accept dual, round-pronged plugs (not shaver plugs). Visitors would do well to purchase converter/transformer kits (in the United States) and/or converter plugs in the European countries prior to their departure.

Time Differences

Greek time is ahead of GMT by two hours. Thus, in the Cyclades, it is 2 hours later than in London, 7 hours later than in New York, 10 hours later than in Los Angeles, but 7 hours earlier than in Sydney. Daylight saving time, in summer, advances the clock by 1 hour.

Geography & Demographics

The thirty-odd islands and islets — 17 officially inhabited — comprising the Cyclades are located in the middle of the Aegean Sea, which is bordered by Macedonia and Thrace to the north, Crete to the south, Turkey to the east, and mainland Greece to the west. Mykonos is located 151km (94 miles) southeast of the Port of Piraeus; Naxos, 166km (103 miles); Paros, 153km (95 miles); Santorini (Thera), 209km (130 miles).

Religion

The Eastern Orthodox Church, a multi-denominational branch of Christianity, embraces Albanian, Greek, Russian, Serbian, Syrian and other religious groups, each denomination self-governing. Greek Orthodoxy is the state religion of Greece and, according to 1977 Greek law, church and state share responsibility in the areas of religion, marriage and the education of the young. The titular head of the Greek Orthodox Church is Patriarch Bartholomeos, who administers his duties from the Ecumenical Patriarchate headquarters in Istanbul.

How Not To Offend

Holidays are associated with greater freedom, and nowhere do holidays seem more liberated than in the Cyclades in high season. This said, a few pointers are in order. Nudity on nude beaches stops where the sand meets the taverna: please don your bikini top before the waiter requests you to do so. Some beaches, and it is quite obvious which, are Greek 'family beaches': please respect the modesty of the locals. When visiting churches and chapels, wear clothing that expresses your respect for the islanders' spirituality: they may tolerate a great deal from their guests, but their churches and often their homes are bastions of 19th-century mores. In general, certain clearly defined areas of the major tourist islands are given over to nudity,

Modesty is requested

high spirits and noise, and areas off the tourist-beaten tracks, march to a different, quite conservative drummer. What's proper on Paradise Beach will not do in the mountain villages of Naxos.

MONEY MATTERS

Banks & Currency

Mykonos: Agricultural Bank, Commercial Bank, Credit Bank, Ionian Bank, National Bank (Monday to Thursday 8am–2pm; Friday 8am–1.30pm; these hours hold for all islands).

Naxos: Agricultural Bank, Commercial Bank, National Bank (all in Hora).

Paros: Agricultural Bank, Commercial Bank, National Bank (all in Paroikia).

Santorini (Thera): Agricultural Bank, Commercial Bank, Credit Bank, National Bank (in Phira, exchange centres in Firostefani and Oia).

The Greek unit of currency is the drachma: in coin, 1, 2, 5, 10, 50 and 100; in bills, 50 (blue), 100 (pink), 500 (green), 1,000 (brown), and 5,000 (greenish blue, and not to be confused with the 500-drachma note). In general, it is wiser to exchange money at Cycladic banks rather than in your home country or at the Athens airport: the rates are better.

Traveller's cheques are the safest way of carrying money. If lost or stolen they can be replaced (within 24 hours in the case of American Express). All Greek banks exchange travellers' cheques, but a smaller handling fee is levied by National Bank of Greece. There is no limit to the amount of foreign currency you may import, but if you intend to export large amounts, register your cash upon entering the country.

Credit Cards

Major credit cards are accepted at most banks, hotels, tourist shops and travel agencies in main towns on the larger islands, but never at tavernas. Often, merchants' prices will come down dramatically when you offer to pay with cash rather than plastic.

Tipping

In luxury restaurants, tipping follows the international standard of 15 to 20 percent, unless the gratuity is added onto the bill. At tavernas, the amount of the tip is at your discretion, but remember that the *mikros,* or 'little fellow' who serves you may receive no salary besides tips, and depend on this money to support himself throughout the year.

Waiting for the exchange

GETTING AROUND

Taxis

Mykonos: The main taxi rank is on Mando Mavrogennous Square in Hora. Throughout the Cyclades, fares are standardised and posted, or cabbies maintain meters.

Naxos: The main taxi rank is in Protopapadaki Square, at the foot of the northern pier.

Paros: The main taxi rank is located

in Ethnikis Antistasis Square, just off the harbour in Paroikia.

Santorini (Thera): In Phira, the taxi rank is located in front of the Agricultural Bank on the main road.

Bus

Mykonos & Delos: There are no vehicles whatsoever on Delos. On Mykonos, there are two bus termini in the main town of Hora. One terminus is located at the crossroads north of the Leto Hotel, and serves San Stefanos, Tourlos, Ano Mera, Kalafatis, Kalo Livadi and Elia. The second terminus is located near the crossroads of the Ornos/Plati Yialos roads,

Kiosks tackle all queries

and services Ornos, Megali Ammos, Plati Yialos (whence the caiques leave for Paradise, Paranga, Super Paradise and Elia) and Psarrou.

Naxos: The bus terminus for southern beaches, hill villages and Apollonas in the north is located in Hora on Protopapadakis Square near the Portara. Naxos buses connect Apollonas, Komiaki, Apeiranthos, Filoti, Chalki, Pirgaki, Tripodes, Melanes, Aghia Anna, Mikri Vigla, Moutsouna, Ag. Prokopios, Maranga, Danakos, Keramoti, Potami and Engares.

Paros & Andiparos: Paroikia's bus terminus is on the port near the small har-

bourside church of St Nicholas. There are five bus routes: 1) Marathi/Costos/Lefkes/Prodromos/Marpissa/Pisso Livadi/Logaras/Chrissi/Akti/Drios. 2) Naoussa. 3) Paras Poros/Ag. Irini/Petaloudes/Airport/Aliki/Ageria. 4) Paras Poros/Ag. Irini/Pounta (Andiparos). 5) Naoussa/Prodromos/Marpissa/Pisso Livadi/Logaras/Chrissi Akti/Drios. The schedule is posted on a kiosk.

Santorini (Thera): Santorini's terminus is located next to the new museum on the main road in Phira. There are eight bus routes: 1) Phira/Perissa. 2) Phira/Kamari. 3) Phira/Oia. 4) Phira/Kamari. 5) Phira/Monolithos/Airport. 6) Phira/Exo Gonia. 7) Phira/Vourvoulos. 8) Phira/Port (Athinios). Buses to Athinios Port leave from Fira, Kamari and Perissa roughly an hour and a half before ferry departures.

Car

Car ferries ply the searoads between Piraeus, Rafina and Lavrion on the mainland, and all the major Cycladic islands. These ferry schedules are available in Athens' travel agencies, or at the offices of the National Tourist Organisation on Syntagma Square. Space must be booked well in advance in order to guarantee passage. Visitors travelling with their own vehicles should be alert to the fact that there are often petrol shortages on the islands in high season. For those interested in hiring cars, the following agencies are reputable:

Mykonos: Mustang Rent A Car, Hora. Tel: 0289 22792/23143/24139.

Naxos: Andonis Koufopoulos Rent A Car, Hora. Tel: 0285 24789; fax: 0285 24345. Auto Rent, Hora. Tel: 0285 24690/24631; fax: 0285 24704.

Paros: Budget Rent A Car, Paroikia. Tel: 0284 22302/23095; fax: 0284 22745.

Santorini (Thera): Drive In Rent A Car, Phira. Tel: 0286 25225/25377; fax: 0286 25377.

Ferries

Ferry schedules are constantly changing, so check in Athens or at the individual ferries' representatives, located on each island. In the high season, boat connections tend to be good and frequent, both to the mainland, to the other Cycladic islands, and, in the case of Paros, to Crete and Rhodes in the Dodecanese.

HOURS & HOLIDAYS

Business Hours

Banks, high season: Monday to Thursday, 8am–2pm; Friday, 8am–1.30pm. General shops: Monday to Friday 8am–2pm and 5.30–9pm; Saturday 8am–2pm; closed Sunday; tourist shops are often exempt from strict regulation.

Pharmacies: daily 9am–1.30pm; 5–10.30pm; late and 24-hour opening, on a rotating basis.

Public Holidays

New Year's Day: 1 January
Epiphany: 6 January
Clean (Ash) Monday: moveable
**Independence Day/Feast of the
  Anunciation**: 25 March
Good Friday: moveable
Easter Sunday: moveable
Easter Monday: moveable
May Day: 1 May
Holy Ghost's Day: 4 June
Dormition of the Virgin: 15 August
'Ohi' Day: 28 October
Christmas Day: 25 December
Boxing Day: 26 December

ACCOMMODATION

The prices listed here are given as a rough guide. They are per room, based on two people sharing, and apply to accommodation in the high season (roughly June to early September), when the Cyclades are most popular. During the other months, you may find you can pay as little as half the amount quoted here.

$ = under 10,000 drachmas; $$ = 10–20,000 drachmas; $$$ = 20–30,000 drachmas.

Mykonos

If you are planning to visit the Cyclades in high season, roughly after Greek Orthodox Easter in April or May till mid-October, book accommodation from your country of origin. Do not disembark with-

'Ohi' Day in the Cyclades

out reservations expecting to find a cheap room, or indeed any room, on Mykonos. What follows here is a brief list of good hotels in several categories, and the name of a trustworthy travel agent who will book space with the hoteliers or make referrals for you should direct communications fail.

All but one hotel listed here are in the Maouna district of Hora, convenient to the capital and well situated for people using this guide. Should you be seeking a hotel on the beach, and more peace than Maouna offers, try the Mykonos Beach and Mykonos Bay hotels on Megali Ammos Beach, five minutes from the crossroads, or the Hotel Princess of Mykonos, here listed, located at San Stefanos Beach.

SEA & SKY TRAVEL AGENCY
Waterfront, Hora
Tel: 0289 22853/24753; Telex: 293 207
SKY GR; fax: 0289 24582
Ask Takis Manesis anything, and mention my name. When you arrive, he will provide you with a special blue-tinted map of Hora, which is essential for getting around.

HOTEL ELENA
Theatraki area, Hora
Tel: 0289 23457/24134/24112/22361;
fax: 0289 23458; in winter, call 0289 24395
Located in Hora, near absolutely everything, the Elena is a quiet, impeccably clean Cycladic hotel with views of the town and harbour. Rooms have TV, A/C, and are heated in the winter, plus there's a great buffet breakfast. Watch the sunset from the veranda-bar. *$$*

A typical Greek view

APOLLONIA BAY HOTEL
Aghios Ioannis, about 3½km (2¼ miles) from Hora
Tel: 0289 27890–5; fax: 0289 27461; in winter, call 0289 24112
This traditionally Cycladic cluster of small villa-studios is located on its own bay. The Kousathanas family are gracious hosts; the view is incomparably lovely. A large swimming pool, in-house bar, and rooms furnished with A/C, TV, hairdryers, etc. are compelling perks. *$$*

HOTEL PRINCESS OF MYKONOS
San Stefanos Beach
Tel: 0289 23806/24735; fax: 0289 23031
Theodore Rousounellos's five-star hotel, located 2km from Hora, 30 metres above San Stefanos's Beach, features air-conditioned rooms and rooms with kitchenettes, 48-channel TV, pool, in-house Italian restaurant and transport to the airport and port. *$$$*

Naxos

CHATEAU ZEVGOLI
Two minutes' walk straight uphill from the port, in Kastro (Hora)
Tel: 0285 22993/24358/24525
Quiet, plush and exclusive, this mansion is the ultimate pension. Great views from some rooms; the honeymooners' room is complete with a four-poster; but no room phones. See owner Despina Kitini at the Naxos Tourist Information Centre, situated across from the bus terminus in Hora. *$–$$*

BARBOUNI HOTEL/BARBOUNIS APARTMENTS
200m (660ft) from Aghios Georgios Beach, Hora. Tel: 0285 22535, 24400, 24401; fax: 0285 23137
This small, family-run establishment is noted for its attentivee service. Stamatoula, the daughter of the family, is a fount of information about Naxos's history and culture. *$–$$*

HOTEL ANIXIS
334 Amphitritis Street, Kastro (Hora)
Tel: 0285 22112/22782
This modest, very Greek, family-run pension overlooks the sea and the Grotta quarter. *$*

Paros

AVANT TRAVEL (and Budget Rent A Car)
On the harbourfront, across from the bus depot, Paroikia. Tel: 0284 22302, 22748; fax: 0284 22745
Marietta Loizos, and Ioannis Kontos, can handle connections, accommodation, currency exchange and all enquiries, with a smile.

VAYIA HOTEL
Two minutes uphill from the port; near the Church of Ekatontapyliani, Paroikia
Tel: 0284 21068; 23335
The Apostolopoulou family runs this immaculate, small hotel surrounded by olive trees and flowers. The second-storey rooms have views of Krios Beach. *$*

HOTEL POLOS
Parallel to the harbourfront, just northwest of Avant Travel, Paroikia
Tel: 0284 22173; fax: 0284 21983
Authentically Cycladic interiors; quiet; upper rooms look out onto the port. *$$*

HOTEL YRIA
2.8km (1.7 miles) outside of Paroikia, on the road to Parasporos Reserve through Avant Travel. Tel: 0284 22302, 22748; fax: 0284 22745
This is a splurge of a place, complete with pool, bar, restaurant, tennis, etc. *$$$*

ROCCO'S STUDIOS
On the port in Andiparos Town
Tel: 0284 61265, 21019; fax: 0284 22731

Chrissoula Patelli's apartments, with kitchenettes, are clean, private and, off season at least, quiet. *$*

Santorini

Santorini can be quite demanding of visitors, who may find they have 3km (2 miles) or 100–200 steps to climb to get home of an evening. Markozannes Tours can arrange accommodation at any of the *skafta* (traditional residences on the cliff face), or in one of the more user-friendly hotels for those seeking less of a climb. Tel: 0286 22813/22987; fax: 0286 23107. In Oia, contact Karvounis Tours.

PHENIX APARTMENTS
On the cliff face in Imerovigli
Tel: 0286 22554/22007; fax: 0286 23809
Christos Vlahoyannis restored these caldera-side studios, retaining the integrity of the 19th-century architecture, but adding 1990s comforts. Ask for 'the Rock Room', where one of the walls is a sculpture of living volcanic rock, or for the studio apartment whose window is a port hole into the swimming pool. *$$*

FANARI
On the cliff face in Oia, beneath the windmill. Tel: 0286 71321/71008; fax: 0286 71235
Barrel-vaulted luxury *skafta* above Ammoudi Bay (the little cove 240 steps down from Oia), this is the nicest place in town. Pool, terrace, and a wonderful bar – the perfect place to watch the sunset. *$$$*

ARCHONTIKO ARGYROU GUEST HOUSE
Messaria.
Tel: 0286 31669; fax: 0286 33064;
e-mail: argyros@compulink.gr
In the family since the 1860s, this exquisite house museum/guest house is a national treasure. (Ask Mrs Argyros for a tour of her husband's ancestral home.) *$$$*

HEALTH & EMERGENCIES

Physicians & Clinics
Mykonos
Health Centre, Hora. Tel: 0289 22274
Health Centre, Ano Mera. Tel: 0289 71395
Dr Loukianos Kouerinis. Tel: 0289 23888

Naxos
Naxos Hospital, Hora. Tel: 0285 23550
Paros
Paros Health Centre, Paroikia. Tel: 0284-22500/1/2/3
First Aid, Naoussa. Tel: 0284 51216
Dr Ioannis Tsigonias. Tel: 0284-22477/23550
Santorini (Thera)
First Aid, Phira. Tel: 0286 22232
First Aid, Emborio. Tel: 0286 29222
First Aid, Oia. Tel: 0286 71227
First Aid, Pyrgos. Tel: 0286 31207

Arrows point the way

Dr. George Vlahos, tel: 0286 24100/71050.

Natural Hazards

The Cyclades are home to both pit vipers and scorpions, the bite of the former being fatal if untreated. The Aegean harbours sea urchins, whose imbedded spines produce nasty infections, and jellyfish, whose stings are more than just a nuisance to nude bathers or those with allergies to their toxins. Seek medical help immediately if bitten by a snake or if you have known sting and bite allergies. The invisible fauna – in the water – are another hazard. After many bouts of summer salmonella, I have given up Cycladic tap water, even for washing my teeth. I also avoid coffee and tea (rarely brought to a boil) in cafés and on ferries, and pack prescription drugs for diarrhoea and nausea.

COMMUNICATIONS & NEWS

Foreign-language newspapers and periodicals are available at any of the newsagents listed below:

Mykonos: International Press and Newsstand, near Church of St Kyriaki in Hora.

Naxos: At the FOTO Service/Foreign Press, halfway down the harbour in Hora.

Paros: At La Palma, adjacent to the Avant Travel Agency on the harbour in Paroikia.

Santorini: At the Argiros Brothers' shop on the extreme northern end of Ypapantis Street in Phira.

Post & Telephone

Post offices are open daily, 7.30am–2pm. Telephone exchanges (OTE) are also open daily, 7.30am–10pm, and international connections are good.

THE GREEK LANGUAGE

The Greek Alphabet

Police

Mykonos
Police, Hora. Tel: 0289 22235
Tourist Police, Hora. Tel: 0289 22482
Harbour Authority. Tel: 0289 22218
Naxos
Police, Hora. Tel: 0285 22100
Harbour Authority, Hora. Tel: 0285 22300
Paros
Police and Tourist Police, Paroikia. Tel: 0284 23333
Harbour Authority, Paroikia. Tel: 0284 21240
Santorini (Thera)
Police, Phira. Tel: 0286 22649
Harbour Authority, Phira. Tel: 0286 22239

Public Toilets

Mykonos and Delos: In Hora, on the harbour near the pier for Delos-bound craft. In Ano Mera, just off the main square: ask at one of the cafés. On Delos, in both the museum and the adjacent café.

Naxos: Near the taxi rank in Hora.

Paros: Directly behind the little blue-domed church of St Nicholas on the harbourfront.

Santorini: In Phira, a block and a half from Theotokopoulou Square, near the Kallisti Hotel.

CAP.	L.C.	VALUE	NAME
A	α	a in father	alfa
B	β	v in visa	vita
Γ	γ	gh before consonants and a, o and oo; y before e, as in year	ghama
Δ	δ	th in then	thelta
E	ε	e in let	epsilon
Z	ζ	z in zebra	zita
H	η	e in keep	ita
Θ	θ	th in theory	thita
I	ι	e in keep	yota
K	κ	k in king	kapa
Λ	l	l in million	lamda
M	μ	m in mouse	mi
N	ν	n in no	ni
Ξ	ξ	ks in jacks	ksi
O	o	o in oh	omikron
Π	π	p in pebble	pi
P	ρ	r in raisin	ro
Σ	σ	s in sun	sigma
T	τ	t in trireme	taf
E	ε	e in keep	ipsilon
Φ	φ	f in favor	fi
X	χ	h in help	hi
Ψ	ψ	ps in copse	psi
Ω	ω	o in oh	omega

Dipthongs

Type	Value
αι	e in let
αυ	av or af in avert or after
ει	e in keep
ευ	ev or ef
οι	e in keep
ου	oo in poor

Double Consonants

μπ	b at beginnings of words; mb in the middle of words
ντ	d at beginnings of words; nd in the middle of words
τζ	dz as in adze
γγ, γκ	gh at the beginnings of words; ng in the middle of words

Vocabulary

Note: This list is broken into syllables, the stressed syllable marked with an accent. Pronounce e as in pet; a as in father; i as in keep; o as in oh.

Numbers

one	é-na (neuter)/ é-nas (masc.)/mí-a (fem.)
two	thí-o
three	trí-a (neuter)/tris (masc. and fem.)
four	té-se-ra
five	pén-de
six	ék-si
seven	ep-tá
eight	ok-tó
nine	e-né-a
ten	thé-ka
eleven	én-the-ka
twelve	thó-the-ka
thirteen	the-ka-trí-a/the-ka-trís
fourteen	the-ka-té-se-ra

etc. until twenty.

twenty	í-ko-si
twenty-one	í-ko-si é-na (neuter and masc.)/í-ko-si mí-a (fem.)
thirty	tri-án-da
forty	sa-rán-da
fifty	pe-nín-da
sixty	ek-sín-da
seventy	ev-tho-mín-da
eighty	og-thón-da
ninety	e-ne-nín-da
one hundred	e-ka-tó

Greetings

Hello	yá sas (plural/polite) yá sou (sing./familiar) ya (abbreviated)
Good day	ká-li mé-ra
Good evening	ka-lí spe-ra
Good night	káli ník-ta
Welcome	ká-los ir-tha-teh
Good luck	ka-lí tí-hi
How are you?	Ti ká-ne-te? (plural/polite) Ti ká-nis? (singular/familiar)
pleased to meet you	há-ri-ka

Getting Around

yes	ne
no	ó-hi
okay	en dák-si
please	pa-ra-ka-ló
thank you	ef-ha-ris-tó
very much	pá-ra po-lí
excuse me	sig-nó-mi
it doesn't matter	then bi-rá-zi
it's nothing	tí-po-ta
certainly/polite yes	má-li-sta
Can I..?	Bó-ro na..?

Signs of the times

89

When?	Pó-te?
Where is..?	Pou í-n-e..?

Do you speak English
mi-lá-te ta an-gli-ka
Do you understand?
Ka-ta-la-vé-ne-te?
What time is it?
Ti ó-ra i-ne?
What time will it leave?
Ti ó-ra tha fi-gi

I don't	then (plus verb)
I want	thé-lo
I have	é-ho
here/there	e-thó/e-kí
near/far	kon-dá/ma-kri-á
small/large	mi-kró/me-gá-lo
quickly	grí-go-ra
slowly	ar-gá
good/bad	ka-ló/ka-kó
warm/cold	zes-tó/krí-o
bus	le-o-for-í-on

boat	ka-rá-vi, va-pó-ri
bike/moped	po-thí-la-to/
	mo-to-po-thí-la-to
ticket	i-si-tí-ri-o
road/street	thró-mos/o-thós
beach	pa-ra-lí-a
sea	thá-la-sa
church	e-kli-sí-a
ancient ruin	ar-hé-a
centre	kén-tro
square	pla-tí-a
Have you..?	É-hie-te..?
Is there..?	É-hi..?

How much does it cost?
Pó-so ká-ni?
It's (too) expensive
I-ne (po-lí) a-kri-vó

How much?	Pó-so?
How many?	Pó-sa?

Emergencies

doctor	ya-trós
pharmacy	far-ma-kí-o
police	as-ti-no-mí-a

USEFUL ADDRESSES

The following local travel agencies are efficient and can be relied upon to arrange travel and accommodation.

Mykonos & Delos

Sea and Sky, Hora. Tel: (0289) 22853; fax: (0289) 24582

Naxos

Naxos Tourist Information Centre, Hora. Tel: (0285) 25200; fax: (0285) 24358
Passenger Tourist and Travel Agency, Hora. Tel: (0285) 24581/22715; fax: (0285) 24581
Naxos Tours, Hora. Tel: (0285) 22043/23743/22095; fax: (0285) 23951

Paros & Andiparos

Avant Travel Agency. Tel: (0284) 22302/22748/23095; fax: (0284) 22745

Santorini (Thera) & Therasia

Markozannes Tours, Phira. Tel: (0286) 22813/22987; fax: (0286) 23107
Bellonias Tours, Phira. Tel: (0286) 22221, 22469, 23604
Kamari Tours, Kamari. Tel: (0286) 31390, 31455, 22890; fax: (0286) 31497
Karvounis Tours, Oia. Tel: (0286) 71290/92/09; fax: (0286) 71291

National Tourist Information

Greek National Tourist Organisation, 2 Amerikis Street, 10564 Athens. Tel: (01) 322 3111; fax: (01) 322 4148
In the US: 645 Fifth Avenue, Olympic Tower, New York, NY 10022. Tel: (212) 421 5777; fax (212) 826 6940
In Germany: Neue Mainzer Strasse 22/6, 60311 Frankfurt. Tel: (69) 236 561/2/3; fax: (69) 236 576
In the UK: 4 Conduit Street, London W1R 0DJ. Tel: 0171-734 5997; fax: 0171-287 1369

FURTHER READING

This list is designed for travellers seeking a deeper understanding of Greece. The first group of titles are best purchased (or located in libraries) in your country of origin; the second are only available in Greece and should be purchased in Athens at one of the following bookshops:
Compendium Ltd, 28 Nikis Street. Tel: 322 1248.
Eleftheroudakis International Book Centre, 4 Nikis Street. Tel: 322 1231.
Reymoundos International Bookstore, 18 Voukourestiou Street. Tel: 364 8188.

Boleman-Herring, Elizabeth, *Insight Pocket Guide: Athens.* 1992 (updated 1997), Apa Publications, Singapore. For those stopping for a short stay in Athens to or from the Cyclades.

Zenfell, Martha Ellen (ed.), *Insight Guide: Greek Islands.* 1991, Apa Publications, Singapore (updated 1996). A well-illustrated, in-depth look at the culture and customs of all the Aegean islands.

Bent, James Theodore, *Aegean Islands: The Cyclades, of Life Among the Insular Greeks.* 1965, Argonaut Inc., Chicago. This is a new edition of Bent's immensely entertaining 19th-century travelogue and anthropological ramble through the Cyclades.

Dubin, Marc S, *Trekking in Greece*, 1993, Lonely Planet. A hiker's guide to Greece, both mainland and island, with a fine section on the Cyclades.

Fitton, J. Lesley, *Cycladic Art.* 1990, Harvard University Press, Cambridge. This is a straightforward, illustrated guide to the beautiful, abstract treasures of the Early Cycladic period.

Morris, Jan, *The Venetian Empire: A Sea Voyage.* 1990, Penguin Books, London. A must for those interested in the Venetians of the Fourth Crusade and their shenanigans in the Archipelago.

Raeburn, Nancy, *Mykonos: A Memoir.* 1992, New Rivers Press, Minneapolis. A painter-poet's seasons in the Mykonian hinterland, this is a richly evocative portrait of the growth of an island under a strong sun.

Books and fruit, Naxos

Holden, David, *Greece Without Columns: The Making of the Modern Greeks.* 1972, J. B. Lippincott Co., Philadelphia and New York. Despite the publishing date, Holden's insightful analysis of the modern Greek state still holds water, Aegean and Ionian.

In Athens:

Boleman-Herring, Elizabeth, *Greek Unorthodox.* 1990, Foundation Publishing, Athens. For travellers who fall in love with Greece (and a Greek) and consider extending their holidays indefinitely.

Paradissis, Alexander, *Fortresses and Castles of Greece: Volume III.* 1982, P. Efstathiadis and Sons, Athens. This little tome is for medieval history buffs and fortress aficionados.

Stone, Tom, *Greek Food and Drink Book.* The handbook of choice for those more interested in kitchen than beach.

Zaphiropoulou, Photini, *Delos: Monuments and Museums.* 1983, Krene Editions. Also available *in situ* on Delos, this is the best guide to Apollo's isle.

Index

ACKNOWLEDGMENTS

The author wishes to thank the following for help above and beyond the call of philotimo: on Mykonos, Takis Manesis and Hazel Fouski; on Paros, Marietta and Loizos Kontos; on Naxos, Stamatoula Margariti and Zorbas Grazias; on Santorini, Christos Vlahoyannis; in Athens, Jenny Colebourne and Paris Raftopoulos. This book is dedicated to the late Elizabeth Janette Boleman Herring Groves, who first took me to the Cyclades in 1960.

Photography	**Markos G. Hionos** and
Page 11	**By courtesy of Ashmolean Museum**
79	**David Beatty**
14	**Benaki Museum**
30, 36, 82, 85, 90	**Elizabeth Boleman-Herring**
10	**Carlotta Junger**
Handwriting	**V. Barl**
Production Editor	**Erich Meyer**
Cover Design	**Klaus Geisler**
Cartography	**Berndtson & Berndtson**